The Pink Ladies Club © 2017

First edition, Rebatesenior Publishing September 2017

The right of Karen Bates to be identified as author of this work has been asserted by her in accordance with sections 77 and 78 of the Copyright, Designs and Patents Act 1988.

Cover Illustration Copyright © 2017 by Karen Bates

Cover Design Copyright © 2017 by Karen Bates

Book Design and Production by Karen Bates and Ashley Reeves

Editing by Sarah Dawes: thankthecat@gmail.com

Find out more about the author and upcoming books on Twitter: @KarenBates64 and on Facebook: /karen.bates.7393

Dedication

It is only through adversity that we find an understanding of what we have been through, and with this, the strongest bonds of friendship are formed.

Without these friendships that have given me hope, encouragement, and kept me going, when at times I just wanted to give up, my treatment would have been unbearable.

Knowing there was always someone who had worn my shoes, walked the walk and had come out the other side, spurred me on. When no one around me knew what to say or how to help, these strong, witty and compassionate women were there for me, every step of the way.

My wonderful pink ladies, whom I now call my friends; my fellow warriors, a band of sisters united by a dreadful disease, forever joined in our own pink ladies club.

I dedicate this book to you.

A note from the Author

This is a personal memoir of my breast cancer diagnosis and treatment.
I am not medically trained and so any information that you glean from my story is not backed up with a warranty from a medical institute. Speak to your oncologist or doctor if you have any concerns.

My intention in writing this book is to offer hope and encouragement to anyone going through treatment, for them or their loved ones.

I have written down how I coped with my diagnosis and treatment and I hope this may be of help to anyone else staring cancer in the face. I am not strong, nor do I have magical powers; I am a woman who was simply thrown into the world of medical treatment by hearing the words, 'You have breast cancer'.

Welcome to the pink ladies club.

* * *

Prologue

I hate pink. It's not my favourite colour - blue is my favourite colour - but because I was born a girl and not a boy, it seems from birth I am supposed to embrace pink.

Everywhere you look pinks symbolises femininity; girls, women, ladies, we are the fairer sex who wear pink and embrace its fluffiness, or so we are led to believe. It's no wonder then that a cancer that affects millions of women worldwide has taken up the pink anthem. You only have to see a pink tutu and tiara with a collection bucket and realize that the fairy within is all dolled up, getting the message across,
 that breast cancer is pink.

My breast cancer wasn't pink, it was a dark charcoal black, so dark I couldn't see out of the tunnel I had unexpectedly been plunged into. There was nothing pink about hearing those words, 'You've got cancer'. There was nothing fluffy about the tumour growing in my left breast. I imagined a blob of missformed cells oozing evil and pus, possibly with little red devil horns for the full effect. No, my cancer was as dark and scary as the ninth circle of Dante's hell.

I have however put all this to one side and embraced my inner warmth, which is pretty difficult to ignore when you're rolling around with your umpteenth hot flush spreading across your whole body at two am. I am now a pink warrior, a survivor, a fully paid up member of the pink ladies club. I should be shining out like a ripe pink lady apple ready to bite into. The black ugly tumour has been removed, my body has been saturated with toxic chemicals; all that is left, I hope, is my pinkness.

Chapter One

* * *

In the Pink

'Have you had your mammogram yet?' I asked my mum.

'No, it's on Tuesday at two thirty in Morrison's car park. When's yours?

'Thursday, ten o'clock at Tesco's. After I'm finished I can pop in and get my friend a present,' I said, 'it's her birthday and we're going round for lunch.'

I had received the invitation in the post to get my boobs squished and as I was working away in Worcestershire I could easily have ignored the letter. It just so happened however that the appointment was on my day off and, with our flat being rented out for the first time, it would be an ideal opportunity to pop home, check out our tenant and make sure the place hadn't been wrecked.

'I think we should go home next Thursday,' I had said, turning to look at Terry. 'A flying visit just to see everything's okay with the flat - and I've got this,' I said, waving my appointment letter at him. 'I think I should go, my mum's having hers.'

'You're not worried about anything, are you?' Terry asked.

'God no! It's routine, I'm fine. I just thought it might be an idea to go home and I could get this done too, or you know what they're like; I'll keep getting reminders until I do go. If it's anything like the cervical smear campaign then they will probably hound me until I make an appearance.

I had no lumps, bumps or signs of anything untoward going on with my breasts. I'd had a mammogram three years earlier - a routine before my hysterectomy - and been given the all clear. Those five minutes waiting in the hospital in Normandy had seemed like the longest in my life. I remember thinking, *how the hell do women in England wait two weeks for the result?*

*

The following Wednesday we were in Devon and after a bit of squashing and turning, raising my arms this way and that, rotating from one side to the other, I was asked if I wouldn't mind filling out a questionnaire. I ticked all the boxes with a relieved smile on my face, giving the mobile screening service ten out of ten all round.

'What happens if I'm recalled?' I asked as I was picking up my handbag and putting my sunglasses on.

'Oh, don't worry if you don't hear anything for a few weeks. If there is anything important, then they usually phone you.'

With that information neatly stored away, I stepped down the metal stairs into the bright light, adjusted my lenses and went off to buy wine and flowers.

Back at work the following day, and relieved that our tenant appeared to have a very bad case of OCD, we had been pleased to find our home cleaner than when we had left it. We settled back reluctantly into work and living away from home. It was July and the campsite where we were working was full. Fridays were always our busiest day and meant that we wouldn't finish until eleven o'clock at night - unless someone managed to do something stupid in the night when we would all be woken to see what was going on. I was worn out; the drive to and from Devon was a long one and our whistlestop trip had taken its toll on me. I climbed into bed that night in our caravan, with the dog on the floor next to me, and fell asleep. Our days were long and although not arduous, the site was going through a renovation programme and nothing was going to plan. Our managers were inundated with complications and delays and as there were only the four of us on the hundred-pitch site, tempers had been frayed. We were all trying to rise above the constant mess and disruption, along with dealing with the campers but it wasn't a happy camp, and the grumpiness was contagious.

The following day my manager, who had also just been home to have her mammogram, asked if I had received my letter yet. It had been nearly three weeks now and as they say, no news is good news, so I had put it to the back of my mind.

'No, not yet.' I said. She had received hers and had been given the all clear.

As if on cue the postman walked in and handed a bundle of letters to me. There it was in the white envelope marked personal and confidential, redirected from my address in Devon.
Opening the letter, I read that I had been recalled, something suspicious had been found and I was requested to attend Exeter breast screening clinic on Friday 15th. Yesterday! I realized I was

supposed to have attended yesterday! I tried ringing the number on the letter, but it was Saturday now and after twelve o'clock, there was no reply, only an answering machine asking me to call back at nine am on Monday morning.

'Shit, shit, shit,' I said unable to contain my panic. What did they mean something suspicious? What the bloody hell did that mean?

'It will no doubt be something and nothing,' my manager told me in her best calming tone. Everyone agreed: a faulty image or blurred screen, or perhaps the machine had broken down and they just needed to take more pictures.

Yes, I thought, *nothing to worry about, it won't be anything. After all, I haven't got a lump and surely you need a lump to have breast cancer.*

Monday morning couldn't come quick enough. I kept telling myself all weekend it was nothing, having a good old feel of my breasts - and getting Terry to join in too. I was convinced it was a mistake. I just needed a doctor to confirm that and I could carry on as normal.

I got through on the third attempt. *Monday mornings must be busy,* I thought, *all those women waiting to ring over the weekend, possibly driving themselves silly with worry.* An appointment was rescheduled and I was told a letter with directions to the clinic would follow.

'No need to be alarmed Mrs Bates; the radiologist would like to take another look that's all.'

'So it could have been a blurred image or a broken machine,' I told

Terry - and most importantly, myself.

Chapter Two

* * *

The Long and Winding Road

The following week we arrived at the breast clinic in Exeter. It was on a side street just off the main shopping area. It didn't look like a hospital. The building was innocuously bland. If you were driving past you wouldn't have a clue that the faceless ordinary building hid a surgery where people's lives were turned upside down on a daily basis.

As we waited in the plush reception area, with up to date copies of the latest lifestyle magazines strategically placed on the low pine coffee table, I couldn't help noticing the posters and display. Little pink bows for sale and collection tins; advertisements declaring *a race for life*, with women smiling and elated, running in pink t-shirts and lycra, declaring, *'Cancer, we're coming for you,'* and, *'Oi, cancer jog on,"* all inviting you to join their pink army. I looked away, preferring to read the latest gossip in *Heat* magazine. I didn't want to join this group of pink ladies, I didn't belong with them, I told myself, as if by distancing myself from their promotional material I wasn't part of it. I wasn't privy to their exclusive club, oh no! Thank you very much, this was one club I defiantly didn't want to be part of.

The room was quiet with the mellow tunes of Radio Two drifting in and out and the rumbling of the coffee machine in the corner. Ladies were coming out of the inner sanctum with smiles, their partners steering them quickly to the exit. I had arrived early and sitting next to me was another lady from North Devon. She too had been invited by the national screening program to have her mammogram at Tesco's car park, and as we waited we swapped notes. Terry with his head in *Farming Today* read patiently, as the woman next to me began to chat.

'About four out of every one hundred women screened are recalled.' She knowledgeably informed me. 'You're more likely to be called back if it's your first time.'

'Oh yeah,' I said thinking, *aye up; someone's been doing their homework.*

'It was my first x-ray since I returned to England,' I told her, 'I turned fifty last October so I expect that's what it's all about.'

'I read on the breast cancer forum,' she carried on, 'that out of four people that are recalled, three of them won't have breast cancer.'

As I scanned around the room taking in the other two women who were waiting my heart skipped a beat. There were four of us in the waiting room.

'Is that true?'

'Yes,' she said, folding her arms to support her chest, 'I read it could be something simple, like a normal breast change or a benign condition.'

'Oh really,' I said, folding up my magazine, placing it on my lap and turning to look at her.

'Anyway, the statistics online say that one out of three people will get cancer in their lifetime,' she added joyfully.

I hadn't been on the Internet — yet. I was already pretty wound up, despite Terry and I trying to convince ourselves that I was going to be okay. We both hoped I would be the three out of four statistics that didn't have cancer, but I'd have been lying if I didn't say we weren't terrified. Mrs Know-it-all was called in before me, and as I waved her a cheery good luck I opened up my magazine again and carried on reading what the Kardashians had been up to.

On my way into the examination rooms we bumped into each other, just as she was putting her cardigan back on, and with a relief that filled her face, she informed me she was fine, nothing sinister had been detected, she was free to go home. *Holy Mother of Mary, my odds are decreasing,* I thought as I gripped Terry's hand harder and entered the room.

They had found traces of calcifications, tiny dots like stars in the night sky. An area of concern had been flagged up from my scan and so they informed me further tests were needed to see what was going on with these pesky spots.

'No lump then?' I asked.
No lump had been detected but they wanted me to have more mammograms, which would be on a more powerful machine, an ultrasound scan, and to be on the safe side a biopsy. A simple procedure, I was told, where they put a needle into your breast and take out a few cells. Gritting my teeth I got on with it, while Terry

was invited back into reception to carry on reading about tractors.

'When will I get the results?' I asked, sipping the cup of tea I had been given. We were now the only ones left in the room.

'We would like you to come back in a week.'

'It's a bit far to come,' Terry said, dunking a chocolate bourbon into his tea. I explained that we were working away and it wasn't easy to change our days off to travel four and a half hours each way for an appointment just to get results.

'Can I phone you?' I asked.

'It's not normal practice; we do like you to have your results with a clinician, in case you have any questions,' she said.

Knowing I didn't have a lump and it was only a few spots, I couldn't see what they might find to change the situation and after insisting that it really was a heck of a long way, she agreed they would telephone me in a week's time at two thirty.

I went back to work feeling positive and put the whole episode firmly to the back of my mind. That is until the night before the phone call, and then I started with the scenarios.

'No news is good news,' Terry said, 'I'm sure if it was anything they would have contacted you sooner.'

Try to stay positive, isn't that what everyone says? *Stay positive.* As if you're really not going to be doing anything but trying your best to be positive. I weakly nodded in agreement; Terry was right.

I didn't sleep well, tossing and turning trying to relax but just as I was about to drift off my mind would dart off into another direction and I was wide awake again. The next morning went slowly. I busied myself with work and customers, doing anything to while away the time. Finally, at two o'clock I could stand it no longer and phoned the direct line I had been given. As we all stood in the campsite office I shut the adjoining door and made the call in private.

'Hello Mrs Bates,' a calm, reassuring voice said on the other end of the phone, 'Now there's nothing to worry about, there isn't any cancer but we would like to make an appointment for you to have another biopsy. It's a vacuum biopsy this time and it enables us to get a clearer picture of what's going on, that's all. I will send you a leaflet out in the post explaining the procedure and if you could bring your husband with you as you'll be having a local anaesthetic in your breast tissue that would be great.' Her Devon accent made me realize I was a long way from home.

I put the phone down and sunk to my knees. It wasn't cancer - she had said so - but I needed a more detailed biopsy, it was all to do with the areas of calcifications.

Terry and my managers had been waiting to hear the news.

'These changes are a precursor to cancer; it's an indication that cancer may possibly form in the future, but that could take years,' I told them. 'They're just being vigilant, that's all. She said it, they haven't found any evidence of anything sinister.'

'Well let's put the kettle on and have a brew to celebrate,' Terry said.

'I do wish she hadn't said there's no need to worry though, as I'm pretty sure that's exactly what I'll be doing until I get the all clear. I wish people simply wouldn't say that, it just makes you tense,' I said, feeling the anxiety rise in me.

Luckily the following day one of my best friends was coming to stay on the campsite. We had arranged it months ago and I was relieved to see her and her children. Elaine was the distraction I needed and as we chatted away about everything but my impending biopsy, cancer had the habit of rearing its ugly head. After all, it was all around us. We both had friends and family that had had the disease and sadly most of them hadn't made the race for life. Cancer had jogged them on, sometimes far too early.

I was glad to have Elaine around for a few days and even with the halo of fear hanging above my head we had a good time. When it was time for her to leave, we said goodbye and she hugged me, telling me everything was going to be all right and that we would catch up soon.
The following week Terry and I made the journey, yet again, to the breast clinic. The procedure wasn't painful, just uncomfortable. I had to lie on my side with my left boob rammed into the screening machine. I was told the instrument, a great huge needle, would penetrate my skin, and skim off some breast tissue from deep inside. With a nurse holding my hand it was over quickly, they had taken about twelve samples.
I agreed again, (I was getting used to this now) to call the following week at half past two for my results.

It was a beautiful summer's day and, wanting to make the most of our day off work and the good weather, I suggested we had lunch in the pub garden around the corner before winding our way back up the M5.

'What did it feel like?' Terry asked.

'Its like an apple corer; it penetrates your skin and takes out a tiny amount of cells. I couldn't feel anything, it just sounds strange, like an air gun going off, you got a gush of air as they pressed the machine.' I said, tucking into my goat's cheese salad. 'It didn't hurt at the time, but now the anaesthetic's wearing off I'm a bit sore,' I said, rubbing my left breast.

*

The following week I went through the exact same routine, although this time I hadn't been sleeping properly since we had returned from the clinic. It was the anxiety of not knowing what they might find in my tissue. I knew I didn't have cancer, but then why all these follow-up tests? The questions flooded my brain and although I had now told all my friends and family who had gone out of their way to reassure me that I was fine, I really wasn't. Only the nurse on the end of the phone at two thirty was going to allay any fears that were now seeping out like sweat on a weight lifter's brow.

After a testing wait, at last, the results were in, they had found more Atypia cells; this is the stage before they turn to cancer, I was told, and because of the amount I would now need an operation to remove the areas of concern. An appointment and map were in the post for me to see the breast surgeon at The Royal Devon and Exeter Hospital on Monday.

Suddenly this all felt very scary. Serious nurse had now replaced the

friendly, chatty, nurse.
That night I turned to Google.

Atypia Cells.

Breasts are composed of lobules, which make milk, and ducts, which carry the milk to the nipple. The lobules and ducts are both lined by two layers of cells. When the cells lining the lobules or ducts grow, the collection of cells is called hyperplasia. Usual hyperplasia poses no risk, but when the cells grow in an irregular pattern they can become problematic. This irregular pattern is known as atypia. Atypical cells are not cancerous but will increase a patient's risk of developing cancer in their lifetime.

I read out my findings to Terry and put the kettle on. I felt a little easier now. It was just a precaution, that's all that they were doing, nothing more than that, I told him as I tried to get a grip and rein in my emotions.

Back in Exeter, and meeting my breast surgeon for the first time, she took us through the options. I could have just the offending area removed and leave it at that. I wouldn't be symmetrical anymore, or as I was quite large busted she recommended a bilateral mammoplasty. This, she told me, would give me a better result and would basically mean taking away part of my left boob with the bad cells in it and then making it smaller and so as not to leave me looking lopsided she would at the same time give me a nice little nip and tuck on my good breast to even me out. I was ecstatic it all seemed so easy! All I needed were a few pre operation routine tests. A letter with an explanation of the procedure and appointment would be posted out to me, but we were looking at about two weeks time, I was told by the reassuring nurse who had been allocated to me. I now had my own breast care nurse. She gave me her card with the direct line phone numbers on it and underlining her name and extension she assured me that she was there for me day or night and if she wasn't then I was to leave a brief message on the answering machine and she would get back to me as soon as possible. I was to go away and not worry. I felt the arms of the National Health Service wrap around me and cloak me in its protective care.

'Well, that went well,' I said to Terry as we marched back to the car park. 'What did you think?'

'I think she's lovely,' Terry replied, dreamily.
I was happy that my young stylish surgeon with her long blond hair, tight black leather skirt and winning smile had given Terry something else to think about, other than slicing up my breasts.

Shaking my head, I said, 'Where do you think she comes from? Sweden? Norway?'

'I don't know,' said Terry, 'but did you see her?'

*

We came back to our flat in Devon the day before my operation. Our lodger was happy for us to stay overnight and had been a godsend while we were racing up and down the country, allowing us to stay in the flat on our numerous hospital visits. He'd offered to move out but knowing it was only a small operation and I would be back at work in a couple of weeks we had agreed that as we all got on okay and the flat was more than big enough, we would muck in together. The company was a diversion and the rent was valued. Travelling back and forward was taking its toll on our energy and our bank balance.

Excitedly, later that night, I went through my drawers tidying up and throwing away all my big bras as I packed my case for the hospital. I wouldn't be needing them after I'd had my op, I thought. Oh no, I was going to be a svelte C cup and I couldn't wait; it wouldn't just be my sexy surgeon raising Terry's pulse, I hoped.

Chapter Three

* * *

Up to the Wire

We left the house in darkness. Not even the seagulls had started their morning squall. Arriving at Exeter just as the hospital was waking up, Terry carried my suitcase with my new pyjamas neatly folded inside as we navigated our way to the pre-operative ward where I would be assessed prior to my surgery.

Mammoplasty is the removal of breast tissue surrounding the tumour to give a good cosmetic result. Sometimes both breasts are operated on, reducing the unaffected breast to attain evenness and symmetry. The scars are usually around the nipple and down into the fold of the breast and so will be hidden by a bra. As the scars fade they will eventually become less visible. At the same time, some or all of the lymph nodes are removed from the armpit. This is done to see whether the cancer had spread to any of the lymph nodes.

I changed into the hospital gown and surgical stockings and had my blood pressure taken. I repeated my name, date of birth and address that many times I was getting giddy. My sexy surgeon shimmied in, in her leather trousers, tight-fitting sweater and biker boots. Taking out her felt tip pen and marking me up, she said, 'So Karen, we'll be taking you down to theatre at about lunchtime.'

'Okay,' I said, feeling my stomach rumble.

'Before we operate we need to place a metal marker inside your breast. This is so that when we are having a look inside we can easily find the area of calcifications that needs removing.'

'Will you be doing the procedure?' I asked.

'A radiologist places a narrow wire into your breast so that the tip lies within the affected area,' she explained.
'Won't it move?' I asked.

'There is a small hook at its tip so that it does not move before the operation,' The nurse who was with her explained, taking my hand and putting her other arm over my shoulder in a vain attempt to make me feel at ease.

I signed all the consent forms and said goodbye to Terry. There was no point in him sitting around waiting for me; after our early start he might as well go home and get some rest, after all he would be coming back the following day to pick me up. I watched the comings and goings on the ward and made numerous trips to the toilet, each time trying to get a glimpse of the running order for the theatre. I could see my name on the list and questioned when I would be going down as it was now well after lunchtime. I was not only starving from not being able to eat the night before, I was becoming uneasy. At last, the nurse came into the ward and made a beeline for me.

'Time to go now, let's get you to the operating theatre.'

'Hold on, aren't I supposed to be having a marker fitted before surgery?' I asked. 'Have you forgotten?'

It seems they had.

*

After a shot of local anaesthetic, the marker was inserted and although slightly uncomfortable it didn't hurt and was over quickly. I was now ready. I was taken to theatre, but just as I was about to lie on the couch my surgeon appeared.

'I'm sorry, but the radiologist isn't happy for your operation to go ahead,' she said, shifting her handbag from one shoulder to the other. She had changed out of her biker gear now and was gowned up in her theatre garb complete with her long blond hair tucked into a little green cap.

It turned out they had been arguing over the correct way to proceed and the radiologist wasn't happy that I would be having a bilateral mammoplasty without further investigation to see what exactly was going on inside my breast tissue. He had put his foot down and insisted that my operation be cancelled and instead I would have a wire-guided incision to have a good look inside. No breast reduction, no bilateral procedure, I was simply going to be opened up and sewn back together.

I was beside myself, all the gearing up for nothing. I had rid my wardrobe of my old hammock huggers. I had eyed up the cute lacy underwear in Marks and Spencer's knowing that in a few weeks of recovery I would have, at fifty, the breasts of a twenty-year-old. I had spent all my life with big breasts and hated it. I dreamed of a nice pert pair that I could slip a t-shirt over and not stop traffic with. It had been a life of people looking at my boobs instead of me and trying to find clothes to disguise my size. I'd been over the moon to be having a reduction. I didn't have cancer; I had been told so many times. This procedure was a precaution, and so I had embraced my vanity and welcomed my new free NHS boob job.

As I sat there in the dimly lit side room they had found for me, accompanied by Reassuring Breast Care Nurse who herself hadn't much idea what was going on, I sobbed. I sobbed with tears of frustration and annoyance, instead of walking out of the hospital tomorrow morning I was now looking at this operation to poke inside me which meant more tests, more cells being sent off for analysis, more follow-up appointments, and most importantly more anxiety waiting for the results. This wasn't the quick fix operation I had been planning for.

'Will this journey ever end?' I wailed.

 My surgeon promised that I could still be scheduled for the reduction and bilateral mammoplasty. I could still have the operation I had been coveting, at some point, but in the meantime, I had to endure surgery and stitches, which meant recuperation and rest.
As they prepared again to take me into surgery and I signed a completely different consent form, I wiped the tears with my hospital gown.

'What about my husband? What about Terry?' I asked. He had driven the hour and a half back home to North Devon. Who would let him know what was happening? Reassuring breast care nurse told me she had tried calling him but there was no reply.

'He won't be home yet, he's probably still driving, you'd better keep phoning him and let him know he needs to come back,' I said, choking back the tears. 'You need to tell him I'm not staying in overnight now, he needs to come back and take me home.'

*

I came round in recovery to see my surgeon standing over me. She told me the operation had all gone well, as I drifted in and out of the drug-induced sleep.

Terry finally made it back and, after a nice cup of tea and a sandwich, and loaded up with medication, I was free to leave. An outpatient's appointment would be sent in the post and I was to rest up and take it easy.

*

The following week we were back at Exeter hospital again for my follow-up appointment. Reassuring Breast Care Nurse helped me into the short cape that I was becoming used to wearing. Taking off my upper garments, I put them into the basket and sat in the windowless room to wait for my surgeon to arrive. It's a busy clinic and as you wait, adjoining doors are opened and closed, as the team goes from one patient to the next. We were bored and fed up at having to attend yet another meeting, it was four thirty in the afternoon and the clinic was hectic and so Terry started taking photos of me in my fetching NHS gown as we messed about trying to kill time and take our minds off the real reason we were waiting in the airless room. Finally, my surgeon accompanied by Reassuring Breast Care Nurse came in, along with my ever-growing file.

I was examined and after a little chitchat, pronounced okay, my stitches were healing nicely. As she pulled up a chair and Reassuring Breast Care Nurse moved in nearer to me and took hold of my hand, my surgeon started to speak.

I don't think I heard much beyond, 'We have found cancer and you're going to need a mastectomy.' Reassuring Breast Care Nurse, rubbing my hand softly, informed me it would be soon, within the next three weeks and a leaflet explaining it all and an appointment would be sent to me in the post.

We walked out into the deserted waiting room; the clinic had emptied while we had been inside. We carried on down through the maze of corridors, walking robotically, gripping each other's hands in silence as we reached the waiting car. It was quiet everywhere now; the busy car park was deserted as our vehicle sat on its own, waiting for us to return.

'What did she mean, Terry?' I asked, confused, as I pulled the seat belt over my bandaged chest.

'She said as they were finishing off the operation, right at the end, just as they were about to sew you up, hiding there at the back of your chest wall they found it.'

'Oh,' I said, not really able to comprehend.

'And I have to have this operation? I can't have a lumpectomy now?' I asked, still dazed and confused and so very glad I had someone with me who had taken it all in and was now able to interpret what had been said.

'Yes, it has to be a mastectomy unfortunately, due to the large area of calcifications. They only found one bit of cancer, but they hadn't looked at everything, so to be on the safe side, they feel the best thing is to remove the whole breast, just in case there's more.'

'I see,' I said, feeling a sickness rise in my throat, listening to my husband who it appeared had suddenly become au fait with doctor speak and terminology, whereas I felt like I had my head stuck inside a toilet roll and a nice fluffy expensive three-ply one at that.

'You have to give it to him,' I said leaning over to grip Terry's hand. 'That damn radiologist who stopped my mammoplasty, he just saved my life.' The man I had been cursing for putting an end to my perky breast dream by insisting on a further biopsy had been right. 'If they had gone ahead with the original operation, then who knows? They might never have found the cancer – until it was too late.' I hadn't been prepared for the change in procedure; it was hard keeping apace of what was happening. 'I had no idea that they could alter your treatment plan,' I said, not really contemplating the enormity of the situation. 'I was really hooked on that mammoplasty op.'

'It's all changed now Kaz; it's the big C we're dealing with now,' Terry said, gripping my hand harder.

It sounds stupid, but I still didn't get it. Cancer, me? Surely not! Someone must have made a mistake. This wasn't on my plan of things to do.

'It's for the best Kaz, at least we know now what's going to happen.' I wasn't sure if he was convincing himself or trying his best to reassure me.

'She's nice,' I said. 'I feel confident with her.'

'I bet everyone says that to her.'

'What that's she's nice?'

'No, not that; when you told her you liked the bacon, don't you remember Kaz? When you asked her where she came from.' Terry said, laughing, letting go of my hand to start the ignition and lightening the mood.

'You can talk,' I said. 'What was all that about? You hoped she was good at needlework as well as science at school?'

'Well let's face it Kaz she's the one going to be sewing you up, I was just hoping she would leave you with a neat little scar that's all.'

Later that week a letter arrived in the post detailing what had been found and an appointment. My mastectomy was scheduled for the twenty-fifth of September - two weeks away. As I read the letter I just wanted it to be over, to be in the operating theatre and have the poisonous tumour removed. I showed Terry the letter.

Oncoplastic Breast MDT Meeting.

Diagnosis: Screen detected 70mm M5calc left breast. Two site biopsies both B4 LCIS Two wire guided local excisions of these areas showed medial pleomorphic LCIS and in the lateral wire, extensive pleomorphic LCIS and on the lateral cavity shave a 5mm area of grade 2 invasive LCIS.

MDT decision Re-excision and sentinel lymph node biopsy with skin sparing mastectomy with delayed reconstruction due to the patient only recently giving up smoking.

Conclusion : The consensus from the MTD is to keep things at this stage as simple as possible to try and conserve as much breast skin on the left as is possible and post-mastectomy to discuss with Mrs Bates-Senior a delayed reconstruction in the future once her treatment is completed and she has been a non-smoker for greater than six months.

*

So there it was in black and white. My life was being mapped out before me; it suddenly hit me that this wasn't going to be as easy as I had thought. This was going to take some doing. A multidisciplinary team meeting had taken place where surgeons, radiologists, and breast care nurses had discussed my biopsies, studied my photos and agreed that this was the way to proceed.

I folded the letter, put the date on the calendar and phoned my mum. Suddenly it all started to feel a lot more serious.

'But you only had pre-cancer,' she said, as if by reiterating my original diagnosis somehow the doctors had made a mistake.

'I know Mum; it's all been a whirlwind of tests, scans and biopsies and every time the ante has been raised. I really thought I had got away with it.'

I had at each appointment been told that what had been suspected had, in fact, turned out to be the worst case scenario and at this point I couldn't work out if this had been a better way of doing things or simply finding a lump, having it verified and knowing right from the start what I was dealing with. The thought that I had been carry on my life thinking I was dealing with pre-cancer had cushioned me to some extent, I had still nearly gone out of my mind with worry, but I had been able to function if somewhat a bit foggy. The anticipation of results had been stomach churning and seemed endless. Every procedure was followed by a waiting time; I had no idea that I would have my treatment changed at every angle.

'They have to take some nodes from my arm pit too, it's to see if it's spread,' I said.

'Oh no, Kaz,' my mum said, exhaling on the other end of the phone. 'I'm sure you'll be fine, Pat next door had a mastectomy years ago and she's okay.'

'Yeah, it will all be over soon and then I can get my life back.'

Chapter Four

* * *

A Bra by any Other Name

There are a few things to be done before a mastectomy operation. You need to have blood taken, your height and weight recorded, a heart monitor and general chat about your health and previous operations. You also need to purchase button-up pyjamas, but mainly it's all about the bra.

Standing in Marks and Spencer's with Terry I looked at the bleak selection of bras that would now be available to me. White, ugly looking contraptions, with inner pockets to put your prosthesis - or pretend tit - into.

'They're awful, I don't want any of them!' I cried.

'You have to buy one otherwise what are you going to come home in?'

The shapeless hammocks hung unflatteringly on an end aisle, tucked away from the bright cerise pink and purple lacy underwired bras that I wouldn't be fitting into for a very long time. As I coveted the sexy balcony range with matching knickers I turned back to the garments on offer.

'This one will have to do,' I said. 'No matching knickers though.'

'I think they must come with those massive beige granny pants over there,' Terry added, 'Do you want some?'

It seems that when you need a post-surgery bra you are suddenly plunged into the depths of the most unflattering underwear available. I was surprised not to see my grandma's skin coloured girdle lurking in the hideous underwear section. I suppose the fact that you don't pay VAT on these necessary articles is something of a blessing at least, although I couldn't help feeling that they should have been free. I mean it's not like they weren't a necessity. I had to have one. I had received a leaflet about what I was required to take into hospital and this was top of the list. My breast care nurse had advised me that the morning after my operation I would be supplied with a softy. This softy would need to be placed inside the pocket of my new bra. It would give the impression that I hadn't gone through a gruelling procedure and that my breast hadn't been lopped off to be analysed in some lab somewhere, along with my nipple. I would walk out of the hospital minus a boob, but no one who wasn't privy to the inside of my underwear would be any the wiser.

'I like these,' I said, holding up a pretty baby blue pyjama set. They were the softest cotton and had little sheep dancing all over them. Picking out matching slippers I took the armful of goods to the counter while the woman on the till processed my purchases with a sympathetic smile. I paid for my things and, swinging the plastic bag from side to side like a petulant child, insisted we went for a drink. I needed a gin and tonic and by the look of it, Terry did too. Bra shopping had never been so exhausting.

The day after tomorrow he would drive me home in my new bra with my softy, and life would be good again. No cancer, no more treatment, I would be over this journey and looking to the future. I had reconstruction surgery to come, but surely this was the hardest bit. If I could survive losing a vital part of me – and oh how vital my beautiful left breast had been in my life - then surely I could survive anything.

Preparing myself, I turned to my online buddies and learnt that with a skin-sparing mastectomy, the surgeon only removes the skin around the nipple, areola and the original biopsy scar, preserving as much breast tissue as is possible. The surgeon then removes the breast tissue through a small opening that is created. The remaining pouch of skin then provides the best shape for your reconstructed breast and can accommodate either an implant or a reconstruction using your own tissue. At the same time, your surgeon will perform a sentinel lymph node removal. The surgeon is then able to tell if any cancer cells have broken away and have travelled to another part of the body. *Holy shit!* I thought, as I read my findings. I hadn't figured it travelling anywhere into the equation. This was the first I'd heard of these lymph nodes. I needed to do more research, ask more questions, to find out what these nodes were all about.

'The sentinel lymph node acts as a kind of watch dog,' someone told me. 'It stands guard for your breast and so the surgeon looks for the very first lymph node that filters fluid away from the breast. If cancer cells are detected here then they are probably breaking away from the tumour and travelling via the lymphatic system.' I now understood: these lymph nodes were the key. If they were clear then my chances of survival would go up, if the cancer had got into and past the watchdog then I could be in trouble. I just hoped and prayed my watchdog was a big German shepherd with gnashing teeth and a scary snarl, not some cute little Labrador that might be caught napping when the rogue cells came a-knocking.

My mum phoned. She'd had a word with her neighbour and had a list of useful things for me to take into hospital.

'It's usually hot, so take some face wipes and a few cartons of juice,' she said. 'You won't be able to get up easily so take some mints to freshen up your breath.'

'I've got new pyjamas, with sheep on,' I told her. 'I read on the forum about having front opening ones, as it's easier to manage than having to keep lifting up your nightie. I've got some bands too for my hair; it's better if I tie it up out of the way. I won't be in long enough to shower - I'm only in one night - so I'm not taking loads of toiletries, just a few essentials.'

'Don't take any valuables or your purse, just a bit of change in case you fancy a newspaper,' my mum advised, sensibly.

I felt like I was off to a spa, not an NHS hospital to have part of me removed.

'Do you know what to expect?' Mum asked.

I told her all about the online forum I had joined and the great advice from ladies who had been through it. My breast care nurse had shown me images of scars, so I had a pretty good idea of what to expect. I was however still anxious.

'It will be good when it's all over and I'm back at home again, Mum.'

'I've put you a parcel in the post, some bits to help you when you get home, and my next door neighbour has popped a card in too.'

Thanking my mum, I put the phone down and prepared to phone my children, both of whom had been total rocks to me, and although miles away were always there at the end of the phone to cheer me up and wish me well.

'I think I've phoned and texted everyone,' I told Terry later on. 'I put it on Facebook in the end as there are so many people messaging me with good wishes. I thought if I put an update on there it would be easier than replying to everyone individually. And I've had some wonderful support, I don't think I could have got through all this without it.'

'It's been a bit of a rollercoaster Kaz that's for sure. I wasn't expecting this at all.'

'I know. I never ever thought I would get breast cancer. I don't know why, but I thought bowel like my granddad or maybe colon,' I said.

'You've thought about it and thought that's what you might get?' Terry asked, amazed.

'Yeah, you know what I'm like when we go anywhere new, like on holiday, sometimes I can't go for three days, well I just thought that can't be good for you, so if I ever got cancer it's probably going to be in my bum as my gut is so sluggish,' I said, pleased with my explanation. 'Breast cancer wasn't on my radar at all and especially after that clear mammogram three years ago.'

'Do you check yourself?' Terry asked.

Resisting the urge to say, 'No I let you do that,' I told him I did, usually in the shower, but I was never obsessed with it; I didn't do it regularly or anything. I had a pretty good idea what my breast looked like and there hadn't been any changes in shape or texture, my nipple wasn't turning inwards and I didn't have any discharge from it. I hadn't felt anything, nothing at all. I felt well, a little tired perhaps, but I had put that down to being back at work after having the winter off and our hectic work schedule.

'And anyway, there was no way my cancer would have been found by a breast exam, my surgeon said the tumour was only the size of the end of your little finger.' I said holding my hand out for inspection. 'It would take some time to grow big enough to feel or see it, and then it might have been a whole different scenario.' I knew this was true and despite being told not to, I had frightened myself half to death with my online findings. Early detection of breast cancer saves lives – fact.

I had a soak in the bath, luxuriating a little longer than usual, pleased to have a lock on the door. We were still sharing the flat with our lodger and, so far, it had worked well. He was discreet and not around a lot and also helped to cook and clean. My daughter joked that we had a slave and he paid us to boot! With my mastectomy scheduled we had agreed he could stay until he had found another flat and so, by the time I came home from hospital, he would have moved out giving Terry and I the place to ourselves. After my bath, I moved my bedside lamp and electric fan to the left-hand side of the bed figuring that this is the side I was to be operated on then it would make life easier for me to turn on and off the appliances. I had tissues and wet wipe to hand and my Kindle and a few books next to my bed. I sorted my drawers out and made sure my new pyjamas were packed along with my loose-fitting top and easy-wear leggings. I made my nest as best I could. Terry said he would change the sheets as it would give him something to do and had agreed to sleep in the spare room giving me plenty of space for me and my drains to get comfy when I returned home.

My daughter, Sarah, had found a charity online that provides women with cushions after breast surgery. She had contacted them and, enclosing a donation, had ordered me one. The heart shaped cushion had arrived the day before, wrapped beautifully in tissue paper and with a little note enclosed. I had been overwhelmed. The beautiful beanbag would slip under my arm, protecting my wound - and I could pop it under my seatbelt for a more comfortable ride home. I picked up the cushion and put it in my hospital bag.

Finally, I scanned around the room that Terry had lovingly transformed for me, knowing that this was the last time I would sleep with my husband with both my breasts.

Things to take into hospital

Face wipes

Shower gel or soap (you probably won't be able to shower so a strip wash with a flannel feels like heaven)

Toothbrush, toothpaste and a little bottle of mouthwash to get rid of that awful taste - and a few mints in case you have a sore throat and to freshen your breath

Dry shampoo is a lifesaver. You may not be able to wash your hair for a while, as it's hard to bend over. Don't forget a hair brush, and bobbles if you have long hair.

Scented moisturiser can often make you feel fresh and clean, but I wouldn't take too many toiletries, just a few essentials. I never wore makeup but if it makes you feel better then go for it! Travel size toiletries are ideal and don't take up too much room.

Things to keep you entertained: magazines and books (although, I didn't feel like reading). I'm a big fan of audio books; you can pop your earphones in and be transported to another world. I found this so relaxing. The only problem was that I had to rewind a few chapters as I inevitably fell asleep.

Phone charger with an extra-long lead. You could set up a contacts group so you only have to write one text or get someone else to let your friends know about you. Messaging and Facebook can be very wearing and answering the same questions over again can be hard work! You are supposed to be resting remember!

A small amount of money. You may wish to purchase a TV card or something from the trolley.

Front-fastening pyjamas and a front-fastening top to go home in, along with your post-op bra. I always wore leggings and either flip flops or comfy slip-on shoes or boots, depending on the weather, to go home in (unless my husband forgot my going home clothes which we won't talk about here...) Hospitals are very warm and when you go back outside again it can be a bit of a shock so make sure you wrap up warm and cosy and have a blanket in the car for the journey home and your heart shaped cushion to pop under the seat *belt. If you have a long way to travel don't forget some water too. You'll feel thirsty and hot – especially if the flushes have kicked in.*

I have saved the most important piece of your armour until last: **laxatives.** *You'll need strong GP prescribed ones, don't mess about with over the counter remedies. I'm telling you, you need the dynamite of the laxative world to free the bunged up mess that the anaesthetic and the shit-load (pardon the pun) of painkillers have blocked up your insides with. The discomfort of not being able to go to the loo is dreadful, so be prepared.*

Chapter Five

* * *

Shit or Bust

This time I was ready for my operation and, it seemed, my surgical team were too, which was an immense relief all round. My surgeon called round to see me and, whipping out her felt tip marker, she proceeded to draw a giant arrow from my collar bone down, indicating it was my left breast that was going to be removed. My right breast had shown no sign of disease; despite lying face down with my tit in a tin can, the excruciating MRI had revealed nothing sinister in my right boob and so at least I would be left with one breast and importantly my nipple could stay. The deafening noise of the MRI scanner and being left in the sterile room alone for thirty minutes had been almost intolerable. You can't move and have to stay perfectly still. As Chris Martin warbled through the headphones it was a relief to finally have some music to listen to after I had put up with Radio Devon's twenty-minute news bulletin. The tears streamed down my face as I held on to Coldplay's words telling me they would 'fix me.'

I had asked if I could have my other breast removed to lessen my chances of the cancer returning, but was informed that they wouldn't remove good tissue with no sign of disease. My right breast would be required to have an annual lone mammogram and I was taught how to exam it with help from my breast care nurse and an over-enthusiastic husband.

'We teach ladies to do this,' she said, stroking the underside of my bosom, 'but in reality, it's quite often the other half that notices something is wrong first.'

'We really should educate our partners to be able to notice any changes,' I replied, thinking it sounded like a great campaign. 'I'm sure the nation would be only too pleased to *feel up* their loved ones, all in the name of medicine,' I said, smiling.

I had been so ignorant and stupidly thought breast cancer was breast cancer. One size fits all. But I was so wrong. I had no idea of the variants; approximately thirty different types of the disease are out there! No wonder women get so confused and GPs often dismiss full-blown cancer for hormonal changes to the soft tissue. I was well on my way to getting a master's degree in anything boob related and was amassing knowledge by the day. The breast cancer forum that I was on helped with my research and it appeared that no question was too dumb to ask. In fact, we were actively encouraged to ask away and usually within a few moments of the post becoming live there would be a dozen women who could empathise, sympathise, or most importantly give advice. At two in the morning, when my brain just wouldn't let me sleep until I knew the answer to a dozen questions, this was indeed a lifeline.

I have found that it is suffering that creates the strongest bonds. Without my pink sisters, I would have struggled along. With them I had the knowledge to march with my head held high, knowing someone had walked, talked and survived the well-trodden path I was being forced to sprint along.

The most important thing I have learned is that breast cancer comes in all sorts of guises and affects all sorts of women and men; from the very young to the elderly, it's a club that is open to all. It appears it's as random as a straw poll. There are no definitive reasons for getting it; some cancers are driven by oestrogen and others don't have oestrogen receptors. Some have the Human Epidermal receptor, Her2 positive and others are Her2 negative; and that's without all the genetic mutations! There are many different combinations and stages of the disease, making most women unique. It is very unlikely that Mrs Jones down the road has the same breast cancer as Doris round the corner, who sailed through it by just taking a few tablets. We are not all the same. Please, if you learn one thing from reading this, don't assume we are all in the same boat. Some of us are in dinghies, some in cruise-liners, and some are paddle-steaming their way along whilst others have sadly missed the lifeboat despite sending out the loudest, scariest and brightest of flares.

They say smoking, drinking, overweight meat eating sloths get the disease, but in my experience, an awful lot of ladies are slim, teetotal, vegetarian, lycra wearing fitness freaks who haven't knowingly allowed a toxic substance to pass their lips. I have made my peace with this knowledge and simply put it down to the luck of the draw. My dad asked me if I'd thought, 'Why me?' and I said, 'Why not me? After all, I'm no different from anyone else and it seems to me there are some pretty amazing women dealing with this diagnosis, so why shouldn't I be part of it?' I'm not sure my dad got where I was coming from, but it sure made me feel better. You see I'm not going to go round wondering what I did wrong, and why I'm here. It's happened and now I have to deal with it. It's not about being brave it's about being brave when you don't have any other choice. It's about choosing to live and choosing to live well. Beating myself up wasn't going to do anyone any good.

As I walked into the theatre for the second time in a month I was upset. I lay on the couch and the tears welled up and started to splash down my cheeks. I have never felt so alone, despite the nurses and anaesthetist who were cracking jokes, I was simply afraid. I knew that the next time I woke up my precious breast would be gone and the cancer with it, but I was in the process of losing part of me, grieving for my womanhood. *I'll be lop sided, a freak with a scar when I awake,* I thought, as the anaesthetist put the cannula into my arm. *A big red ugly scar in place of my boob* I contemplated, as I started counting backwards and drifted off to sleep.

*

Awake and sipping tea, the pain was minimal. I still had on my hospital gown and surgical stockings and it was dark outside. I slipped in and out of sleep and managed to phone Terry and ask him to text my family to say I was feeling okay. Living so far away, we had arranged that he would come and fetch me the following day. I was left to rest and start the process of recovery. I made it to the bathroom, but beyond a wee and washing my hands I didn't feel up to any further preening. I got back into bed and after more heavy-duty drugs, which I welcomed with open arms, I slept a peaceful night's sleep relieved it was all over.

My breast along with the tumour had gone – I was in effect, cancer free.

*

The worse thing about hospitals must be being woken up at an ungodly hour only to be poked, prodded and fed more painkillers. I managed my breakfast and was enjoying the relaxation when the rudest nurse I had yet to encounter started bullying me to get up and get dressed. I started to cry. I hadn't seen my chest yet and this woman was making me take off the hospital gown I had been clinging onto like a security blanket. She wanted me to put my mastectomy bra on, complete with softy that I had been given the day before and she wanted me to do this on my own, behind the curtain with a room full of women. Where was my breast care nurse who, I had been promised, was going to hold my hand every step of the way, I wondered aloud.

'It's Saturday, the breast care nurses don't work on Saturdays, you just have to get on with it, come on chop-chop, hurry up.'

I was devastated they had lied to me. There was no reassuring breast care nurse to help me into my post-surgery bra. No cheerful reassuring face to ease my discomfort and help me look at my savaged body for the first time! This awful bossy nurse expected me to get on with it on my own. The tears were flowing freely now and I was getting in a right mess with the drains, tubes and bottles getting tangled in my underwear. I really didn't know how to put the front-fastening bra on without yanking out the plastic tubes, sending blood and pus flying around the room.

My left arm felt like lead. I'd had my lymph nodes removed and the pain under my arm was stopping me from lifting it very high. Along with the scar on my chest, I felt incapacitated but this evil ogre was insisting I dress myself like nothing had happened to me. Emotional, exhausted and pained, I was relieved when a kind lady in the bed opposite who had recently undergone a hysterectomy hobbled over to assist. Sobbing and holding onto her she got me to look at my body for the first time and helped to dress me, finally fitting in my new cottonwool boob. I have never been so thankful for the kindness of a stranger. I will never forget what she did for me.

Nasty Nurse came back and I told her how mean I thought she had been but I think she quite liked her role and wasn't going to give it up in a hurry. I knew I would be having words with the breast care team though. *If this is her bedside manner*, I thought, *then it stinks*. No one should be treated like that. I was determined to make sure everyone knew, as I couldn't bear the thought of anyone else having this awful woman treat them the way I had been treated.

Terry arrived and I couldn't get away from Nasty Nurse quick enough. As if it wasn't bad enough having to surrender part of your body, I could have done without Miss Bossy Knickers making it doubly painful with her strict unfeeling attitude.

Back at home, my mastectomy pillow tucked under my arm (they really are fantastic for keeping seat belts off your chest) I was tucked up in my own bed with no Nasty Nurse to boss me around, just my well-meaning husband who brought me to tears. This time from the exercises I was given to do. Who would think that just bringing your elbows together in front of you could be so painful? The pain was tough but he pressured me each day to do the required routine and despite nearly fainting and having to sit down to finish them I persevered and glad I was too. Another wonderful side effect from breast cancer is the risk of lymphedema. Again I had no knowledge or idea about this debilitating condition.

It's as if cancer just can't stop giving. Reading the leaflet about it, I could appreciate what Terry was doing for me as lymphedema can be caused by cancer or develop as a side effect of treatment. It is a condition that can appear months or even years after your cancer treatment has finished. It can be as a direct result of surgery to your lymph nodes or radiotherapy to your lymph nodes. It can affect different parts of the body, especially the arms and legs. Not everyone who has surgery or radiotherapy to the lymph nodes will get lymphedema. If, however, you are at risk there are a few things you can do to reduce your chances of developing it.

Look after your skin and moisturise, moisturise, and moisturise. Avoid getting cuts or scratches and know the signs of what to look out for. Make sure your nearest and dearest are aware that you are at risk (in an accident you might not be able to tell anyone yourself). Look out for signs of infections and make sure you get any treated quickly. Keep active and exercise, which will stimulate the flow of lymph fluid in the body. Take care when travelling. Move around and stretch regularly, and wear comfortable clothes and shoes and, finally, if you feel unwell always seek medical help.

*

The drains were still filling and so remained in, with the district nurses calling daily to empty them. It was good to have that contact, as I didn't feel so alone. I felt there was always a trained professional to ask and if I had any concerns a nurse was always only a few hours away from visiting. They changed my steri-strips and emptied my drain bottles and cheered me, telling me I was doing really well.

I received a mountain of cards, flowers and well wishes from friends and family and felt completely spoilt. My mum's elderly neighbour, who had had her own battle with breast cancer and was on the winning side, had sent me a letter with some money in it to treat myself. My wonderful friend Elaine sent me Laura Ashley vouchers and I had been able to purchase new curtains for my newly decorated bedroom before my operation. I truly appreciated all the good wishes and lying in my bed, looking at the cards and flowers, I felt loved.

I spent most of the time in bed and a walk to the toilet, a quick strip wash and eating my dinner were about all I could and wanted to manage in the first week. My chest was sore but the pain medication did its job so I wasn't in any great discomfort. The drains were the worst things - you only forget that you have them in once! Getting in and out of bed and sitting on the loo and at the dining room table, I became an expert at arranging the tubes so that they didn't pull on my skin. The little canvas bags that the hospital had provided me with really helped but I have heard of women carrying them about in plastic bags and even a cardboard wine carrier, but I do recommend the cotton ones. If your hospital doesn't provide them then you can order them from Drain Dollies.

Despite being able to do absolutely everything else for me, my beloved husband just couldn't face washing my hair. I used the dry shampoo but, by the time my mum and dad arrived to stay the following week, I was really ready for shampooing. Terry could manage most things but somehow he just couldn't get his huge hands to wash my hair without bashing me round the earhole, drenching me and my bandages with water, or simply getting shampoo in my eyes. He was a dead loss, and so I called in the expert and my mum came to the rescue. A good tip is to wear an old t-shirt, the water will catch mainly on here leaving your bandages dry, or as one friend did wrap yourself up in Clingfilm –

the choice is yours but try not to get the bandages wet, and if you do, a hairdryer on a low heat setting will dry them out quickly.

It was so good to see my parents and although not out and about we were able to spend a few days inside chatting and enjoying each other's company. My chest wall felt sore and tight and I was still popping painkillers like candy. I was, however, getting used to the bra with the softy in and happy to have the mastectomy behind me. Showing my mum the scars wasn't easy, I wanted her to see but I didn't want her to feel sorry for me - I couldn't handle that. I had just about got my head around losing my boob but I couldn't bear my mum mourning for it too. So I acted matter of fact. A few tears seeped out but I was determined not to let it get the better of me and steadfastly swallowed them back.

The following week my kids came to stay and as I got dressed I showed Sarah my scar. She took it really well and was complimentary about my surgeon's needlework. It made all the difference to have her react so matter of factly. I was grateful my new body didn't upset her and she appeared to be handling it all very well.

I made it outside for the first time; living in a flat wasn't easy, especially when the flat was on the top floor, without a lift. Navigating the stairs, we went for a walk and had Sunday lunch in a pub. The pain was there, humming along in the background, but nothing to moan about. I was well and truly on the mend. I felt great. Despite snitching up Nasty Nurse, everything went well with my follow-up appointment. I did raise my concerns that it seems strange to do mastectomy operations on a Friday when the breast care nurses aren't around at the weekend.

I had now joined another club. I was now officially a cancer patient and was entitled to the benefits of our local charity that ran a help centre at the hospital. To me, this meant a decent cup of coffee in comfy chairs and toilets that didn't smell like an old bedpan. Travelling so far from North Devon to Exeter inevitably meant we were always early as I hate being late, so at least a pit stop at Force was a welcome respite from the draining hospital. It was difficult not to scan around the waiting rooms and take in the short haircuts and tight fitting hats knowing what was going on with them. I still had my long hair and to the outside world, I didn't look like a cancer patient. I didn't have a sticker on my coat declaring me going through treatment. To the passer by in the street I looked well and healthy.

My sexy surgeon, who was today wearing a very tight leather skirt and a figure-hugging t-shirt, proposed me fit and ready for the world. I was free to go. With an annual mammogram in July next year, I needed no further treatment. I should be fine, she reassured me. The surgery had done its job. No other tumours had been found and importantly the cancer hadn't travelled to my lymph nodes, making it much more unlikely to have spread to anywhere else in my body. *My watchdog has done its job*, I thought.

Relief flooded the room as Terry and I hugged each other. I think it's only when you get the results that you really understand just how pent up you have been waiting for them. Breast cancer is a waiting game and as patience isn't one of my strongest points I had had to deal with this awful state trying to be the usual bubbly me, but when I was alone worrying myself sick about worst case scenarios. Nothing is as sweet as hearing those words, 'No further treatment is needed'.

Despite my stitches, we skipped back to the car and happiness. I would be referred to a plastic surgeon that I would see in three months' time and we would be able to start talking reconstruction surgery. My surgeon had agreed I was an ideal candidate for a DIEP flap and would refer me.

'Well, that went well,' Terry said, as he navigated the M5 sliproad.

'I'm so relieved to be out of there, and pleased she is going to refer me to the plastic surgery team to get my new boob,' I said, excitedly.

'Do you think she always wears leather?' Terry asked.

'No, I've seen her in her scrubs,' I replied. 'She still looks beautiful though, even in the shapeless green clothes; she really is very stylish. Mind you, I bet I could be if I were on her wages.' I thought for a second. 'Although I got fired for ducking into the toilets at the first sight of blood when I was a dental nurse, so I don't really think I would have been any good as a doctor let alone a surgeon,' I added, switching on the car stereo. It came to life with Coldplay playing *I will fix you*. I changed the station.

Chapter Six

* * *

Life Gets Back to Normal

I continued to heal well and with no complications, so we decided a short break away would be good for us both. With the constant strain of waiting for results, having the results and then having to act upon the results, we were both pretty peed off with my brush with cancer. I had booked us into an apartment in Looe, Cornwall for a few days respite.

'A bit of sea air will do us some good,' I said, packing my suitcase.

'We live by the bloody sea Kaz! Why do we have to spend money to go and stay by the sea?'

'Because it's a different sea.'

Emotionally I had got over my recent surgery well and had come to terms with my scar. I wasn't worried about how I looked either with my clothes on or off. I was comfortable in my husband's presence and I had simply decided pragmatically that this was how I was now and so for the foreseeable future I only had one boob – but it wasn't going to get in the way – if you'll excuse the pun.

A few days before our trip away I had an appointment back at Exeter hospital with a woman from the prosthesis company who would be providing me with a more 'realistic' false boob. The appointment didn't start well. For some unknown reason, this lady refused to let Terry come into the fitting. He had been my sense of reasoning on all my appointments so far and had been my emotional rock through it all. She was adamant he must wait outside. This large bosomed woman who flashed her cleavage like a threat set to work with her skin coloured jellies. She assured me she would find one that would fit perfectly.

As I got in the car afterwards I started to cry.

'That was the most humiliating thing I have had to encounter so far,' I said.

Terry just looked at me as I explained. It had been downright weird this stranger fiddling with my breast after I had stripped to the waist, trying to size up the rubber blancmange she was squeezing into my pocketed bra.

'It was awful; I felt violated. With her pale blue two-piece on she looked more like a civil servant than a medical person. It was all wrong!' I complained. 'After not so much as, "Nice day, lovely weather for it!", she was looking me up and down, assessing my boobs and messing with my nipple. I'm telling you, Terry, I nearly walked out – in fact, I wish I had done. And look at this bloody thing,' I said pushing my new NHS prosthesis at him. 'It's gross! I hate it. It looks too real.'

'Isn't that what it's all about?' Terry responded sympathetically.

'No, I don't want it to look real! I want my softy back. I don't want this blob reminding me of the flesh I've had cut off; it's so medical!'

That was the nub of it: the fake boob was just too realistic, too skin coloured, too anatomically correct - too much like the breast I had lost.

That night, on the phone, I told Sarah all about my discomfort and how I had felt so humiliated.

'It was like she was selling me lipstick or something and she had massive knockers too, adding insult to injury. Having her breasts pushed in my face, I felt like a cripple.' I wailed. Sarah, after a few minutes, found the solution. A quick search on Facebook and she had found volunteers who made prosthesis. These were knitted so like my softy, but in pretty colours. They did the job but they didn't pretend to be boobs. They were friendly alternatives to the beige lump I had been given. Taking my size, she ordered me one, and an aqua one too; it seemed they even catered for swimming and I loved swimming. Thanking her, I put the phone down and went off to tell Terry my happy news, and eagerly awaited the arrival of my knitted knocker and its twin aqua-knocker.

The post arrived just as we were packing the car for our trip away. My parcel had arrived beautifully packaged with a little note. I welled up inside and played with the attractively knitted knocker. *Now this*, I thought, *this is something I could live with*. I wasn't an old granny; this purple and lilac knitted prosthesis was vibrant and fun. I slipped it into the pocket in my bra and tossed my softy in the bin. This was the new me from now on. I looked in the mirror, you couldn't tell it wasn't a real breast; you couldn't tell it was only made out of wool with some stuffing. The huge rubber prosthesis that weighed a ton was never going to be worn I realized, smiling; this was my new alternative boob for the foreseeable future. We were still young(ish) and had our whole lives ahead of us. I knew I could wallow in self-pity and worry, or try to put it behind me. I chose to put it behind me. As life is for the living, six weeks out of surgery we were heading off down the M5 although this time we wouldn't be coming off at the junction for Exeter. We were going on holiday.

'I think I may have overdone it a bit,' I said that night at dinner. 'When we turned up I never thought I would be able to do so much. I've surprised myself.'

'You've walked miles, Kaz, you've done well.'

'I was determined to do it. I wanted us to have some normal time again. It's been all about me and bloody hospitals; I thought it would be good to have a change of scenery and get away from all that for a bit,' I said, trying to conceal the burning pain in my chest. Nothing was going to stop me having a nice time with the man I loved, I thought as I swallowed more painkillers. We had finished working for the caravanning club by now and were living on our savings. We had contracts to go back to work in the spring and just about enough money, if we were careful, to tide us through the coming months. There wouldn't be any fancy holidays to far off Caribbean shores this winter.

'We'll get back to work in March and start saving again. We can always have a holiday when we finish next year,' said Terry, ever practical.

'It does seem like a long time to wait though,' I replied, wistfully. 'Bloody cancer spoiling all our plans.'

Cancer is like a wasp: it comes and bites you when you least expect it to. What you don't realise at the time is that it is usually pretty damn inconvenient. Nor do you realise just how long that sting will take to heal. When I was first diagnosed I had this mad notion that it would be dealt with quickly and that I wouldn't have had to have quite so many scans, test, biopsies and surgeries to get me to where I was now. The last three months had been a whirlwind of appointments and hospital visits. And now I was going to have to put my life on hold yet again.

'Just think, said Terry, 'this time next year we'll be finishing work at the end of summer with a load of money stashed in our savings and we can have a proper holiday.'

We clinked our glasses in a toast to good health and tucked into our dinner.

*

A few weeks after we returned, as we were on our way into town to meet some friends, I picked up the post from our box. I popped the letters into my bag, to read when we reached the bar.

Nursing my orange juice, I opened the letters addressed to me. The first was an appointment for December to meet with my plastic surgeon to discuss breast reconstruction surgery. The second letter was more ominous.

'I've got to see an oncologist at Barnstaple hospital, Terry. It says my treatment plan has changed,' I told him, my voice shaking. It didn't take a brain surgeon to work out that receiving a letter out of the blue telling me my treatment plan had been changed and that it was with a doctor who specialized in oncology wasn't a good sign. 'Oncology, that's cancer, right?' I asked my friends. 'What do they mean, telling me my treatment plan has changed? I don't get it,' I said, confused.

Later that night, after numerous phone calls to Exeter and Barnstaple hospital and my GP's surgery, my surgeon phoned me. Apologizing for the late reply to my garbled answer machine message she explained she had only just finished in theatre.

'I'm sorry Karen, but your tumour was sent off to be tested at the pathology lab and the results show you will need further treatment,' she said.

'Further treatment? What do you mean further treatment? You mean chemotherapy don't you?' I asked.

She told me that she had referred me to the oncologist and she would explain my new treatment plan at the appointment in a week's time. In the meantime, I was to try not to worry but, she said, it would be a good idea for Terry to be at the appointment, as there might be a lot of information to take in.

I turned to my online forum buddies who would hopefully be able to help. The consensus of opinion was that I was going to be having chemotherapy and to try not to worry.

Breast cancer is fraught with worry at every turn. If the damned tumour doesn't kill you, then the unease that it provokes does a bloody good job of trying to push you over the edge. As soon as you are diagnosed you acquire new two new mates: anxiety and fear.

Like clingy new best friends, you can either choose to hang out with them or tell them to bugger off. The choice is yours. How you handle your diagnosis is unique to you, and anyone who tries to steer you away from spending time with them, or tells you to think positively, can quite frankly 'do one.' Until you have been there you just don't get it, so don't bother with the platitudes. But at some point you have to make friends with them as they simply won't go away.

My advice to anyone whose friend or family member is dealing with cancer is just be there for your loved one. Actions speak louder than words and I would say this is one of those times when you can excel at this. I'm often asked by people whose loved ones are going through treatment what can I do? What should I say? And it's not always easy to get it right, but if you follow a few of the tips I have picked up, then hopefully you and your loved ones will still be speaking long after treatment has finished.

One of the most important things I've learned is that a cooked meal will never be turned away; it will always come in handy, along with helping with child care, school pick-ups or simply asking, 'How is your treatment going?', without offering advice. By asking, 'What's up?' instead of 'How do you feel?', you'll be more helpful. Remember, we might have cancer but we still have real emotions too, so don't wait for your friend to call; after all, we're using up most of our energy fighting to stay alive. Pick up the phone and text every once in a while, making sure your texts don't need an answer as it can be exhausting replying to well-meaning questions.

If you set up a date to meet it might be all that is needed to turn a shitty day into a good one, but DON'T let your friend down as this may be the highlight of their week and an awful lot of effort would have gone into making sure they could attend! Asking someone who has cancer to call if ever they need anything is kind, but it probably isn't going to happen. It's hard asking for help with simple jobs that you used to be able to do. Asking for help may make you feel weak and needy or you might simply be afraid your friend/family will say no, so don't wait to be asked. This is the time to put your money where your mouth is. This is the time to stand up and be counted. If you want to help then do it, don't just talk about it. We are fighting a life threatening disease - we don't have the energy to make decisions for ourselves - so don't make us make choices. After all, given the choice, we would probably prefer to hide under the duvet and block out the world.

You can do small acts of kindness, which will make a world of difference believe me, even just a hand putting out the washing, or helping to change the bed sheets would be so welcome. Honestly, when all you can do is make it from the bathroom to the sofa and back again any help is welcomed and anyway who doesn't love a good natter and a coffee? Just make sure you don't wear the patient out – little and often is the best way to help. But don't forget we need to voice our fears too and if you're a best friend then that will be so much easier than offloading to a partner, parent, or grown up child. Family might be terrified too and not want to listen to your concerns seeing it as a weakness; after all, aren't we told on a daily basis to stay positive? You offer that safe haven for your loved one to express themselves without judging, as believe it or not we do need to fall apart occasionally. Being able to have a good cry is important. It doesn't mean we are weak, it means we are working so very hard to stay strong and that in itself is exhausting! Having someone to let down the barriers with is a vital part of our support structure, so don't be alarmed; it doesn't mean we've given up, it just means we need an outlet too.

If you follow a few of these insights you won't go far wrong. Just listen and don't offer solutions. A good cry is sometimes all that is needed. Cancer treatment is gruelling both physically and emotionally. Sometimes we need to be alone; this brave face we are wearing comes at a price. Sometimes we just need to drop it for a while and recharge our batteries, so don't take the hump if we need a bit of time alone to recharge our batteries. You are the best and if we forget to tell you, be assured that we love you for being there at the darkest point in our lives.

*

Sarah had come to stay and, after a fretful few days, we found ourselves back at Exeter hospital. We had come prepared. Terry had a list of questions (in case I forgot) and Sarah would be taking notes.

'Your tumour has been analysed and it's come back oestrogen positive, which is a good thing as we can treat that with hormone tablets to block its production but more importantly, it's what we call Her2 positive.'
The oncologist went on to explain that this type of breast cancer is aggressive and so they wanted to treat it with an injection. Eighteen injections, every twenty-one days but in order for the injection of Herceptin to work to its full capacity, it was advisable to have chemotherapy alongside it. I was, however, borderline and so the decision to have chemotherapy was my choice. I asked what my oncologist would do.

When someone tells you that you have had an aggressive tumour removed and that with this prognosis your cancer is more likely to return, your head starts to spin. I was grateful that I had Terry and Sarah were with me, it was all starting to sound like white noise. All I could think to ask was will I lose my hair?

'Yes, on this cycle you will.'

'So she doesn't have to have chemotherapy if she doesn't want to?' Terry asked. I could sense he was now getting uptight and agitated. 'What else can you do? There must be other treatments available?' he asked with an impatient snort, unable to accept the enormity of what the consultant was saying.

She went on to explain that, in her opinion, chemotherapy and Herceptin were the best chances of targeting stray cancer cells that might be lurking in my body.

'But her nodes were clear, you said no lymph node involvement. That means it hadn't travelled out of her breast tissue,' Terry said, now clenching his jaw and getting so angry I really thought he was going to take a swipe at her.

'It's just to be on the safe side. You see, it's like a sneeze and if any of the cancer cells got blown off they can settle in your body - usually your bones, liver, or brain - then in a few years' time when no one is looking and you think it's all over, they rear their heads again. That is metastatic cancer and at this point it is not curable, we can only treat it.'

'Bloody hell,' I said, 'when can I start the chemotherapy?'

'Well, we were hoping very soon, in a day or two?'

Everything went very quickly from then on. Reassuring Breast Care Nurse held my hand and Sarah was given a load of leaflets. After a phone call, I was told an appointment had been made for my first session the following day. I would be having four cycles of chemotherapy along with my first Herceptin injection.

As we left the hospital and got into the car my mobile rang. It was a cheerful nurse from Barnstaple's chemotherapy ward inviting me to visit later on as they had a load of information to give me before I went in the following day. Armed with the leaflets, Sarah and I started to read about the treatments.

HER2 (human epidermal growth factor) is a protein that can affect the growth of some cancer cells. It is found on the surface of normal breast cells. Some breast cancer cells have a very high number of HER2 receptors. The extra HER2 receptors stimulate the cancer cells to divide and grow. When there are higher levels of the HER2 protein in a breast cancer, it is called HER2 positive breast cancer.

The higher the level of HER2, the more likely the cell is to grow and divide. Between 15 and 25 out of every 100 women with breast cancer (15–25%) have HER2 positive cancers. Fewer men with breast cancer are thought to have HER2 positive cancers.

HER2 positive breast cancers tend to grow more quickly than HER2 negative breast cancers. However, effective treatments called targeted (biological) therapies have been developed to treat HER2 positive breast cancer. The drug most commonly used is trastuzumab, commonly known as Herceptin.

Chemotherapy

Chemotherapy uses anti-cancer (cytotoxic) drugs to destroy cancer cells. Chemotherapy can be given in combination with trastuzumab.

You may have chemotherapy after surgery to reduce the chances of breast cancer coming back. This is called adjuvant chemotherapy.

There are different groups of chemotherapy drugs. HER2 positive breast cancer is often treated with chemotherapy drugs called anthracyclines and taxanes as well as some others. You'll usually have a combination of two or more chemotherapy drugs.

Targeted therapies

Trastuzumab (Herceptin)

Trastuzumab is a type of drug called a monoclonal antibody. Monoclonal antibodies are sometimes called targeted therapies because they work by 'targeting' specific proteins (receptors) on the surface of cells. Trastuzumab locks on to the HER2 protein. This blocks the receptor and stops the cells from dividing and growing.

It is usually given following surgery and chemotherapy for primary breast cancer to reduce the risk of the cancer coming back. Even if you have a very small cancer that has not spread to the lymph nodes, your doctor may recommend treatment with trastuzumab.

Because it can affect the way the heart works, you will have tests to check your heart before, during and after treatment. Some people with a history of heart disease or uncontrolled high blood pressure may not be able to have trastuzumab.

You can have trastuzumab as a drip into a vein (intravenous infusion) or as an injection under the skin (subcutaneously). It is usually given once every three weeks. If you have early breast cancer, you will usually have trastuzumab for a year. If the cancer is advanced or has spread elsewhere in the body, you will have trastuzumab for as long as it is controlling the cancer. Side effects *tend to be mild and include flu-like symptoms, diarrhoea and headaches.*

The Internet is awash with horror stories and worst case scenarios. It's hard not to frighten yourself half to death with some of the tales and websites. Now I'm not going to say don't Google it because, like a child putting his hand in the fire, you will Google it. It's human nature to be inquisitive and find out as much as you can about what's going on. What I will say is pick your sources carefully. Accredited sites that are based in the UK are more accurate if you are being treated in the United Kingdom. Macmillan and breastcancernow.org are up-to-date and give you a better picture than random searches on Dr Google. And importantly don't Google at bedtime; it's a recipe for spending the next four hours trying to decipher just exactly what was meant. You will do your head in; believe it from someone who has done it.

Chapter Seven

* * *

Chemo Heroes

Seamoor unit at Barnstaple hospital was shiny, new, and very modern. I don't know quite what I expected, but I didn't expect it to be light and airy with music playing in the background and surprisingly happy, smiling faces. The words 'chemotherapy ward' had conjured up a dark room full of scary machinery and sick, hollow looking patients: somewhere you really didn't want to hang out. A bit like I imagined death's waiting room would be.

The friendly receptionist checked me in and after giving me yet more leaflets and paperwork explained what would happen the following morning. It would be a long day as I would need a heart scan to make sure my heart was ok and to measure the vessels, as Herceptin can cause damage to the heart (oh the joys!). I would be monitored every three months to make sure the drug wasn't damaging my heart. I would also need to be observed for longer on my first treatment just to make sure my body was coping and I didn't have any nasty reactions.

We said goodbye after a quick look round and made our way home. Still in shock, I put the kettle on. I felt like I had no choice but to have the chemo. After all, I wanted to live, I wanted to give conventional medicine its best shot at curing me, but Terry wasn't convinced. A few years ago we had seen a good friend who, having cancer, had had chemotherapy and he had looked ravaged by the disease. It was hard not to forget how ill he had looked.

The following day Sarah drove me to the hospital. As she was at home it was decided that she would be better company and more entertaining than Terry. We had packed books, magazines, snacks, a comfy blanket and drinks. It was like going on a picnic, I joked. I had no idea what to expect and apprehensively we entered the hospital trying as best we could to put a brave face on it.

My heart scan was first and was a simple procedure made easier by the fact that I didn't have a breast to get in the way. It was all over and done within fifteen minutes and we walked back to the chemotherapy ward in silence.

We were welcomed onto Seamoor ward and asked where I would like to sit, with a choice of reclining chairs or beds to choose from. We made ourselves at home. A nurse came and explained what would happen. The room was half full, mostly with men and older ladies all hooked up and having treatments. Some were dozing off and others were chatting with their companions, but no-one looked in pain or distress. I thought this was a good sign.

Eventually my poisonous concoction arrived and I was fitted with the needle and wired up to the pumping machine.

'Don't be alarmed, but we give you a steroid drug that makes your bottom itch first,' I was told. 'It's like having ants in your pants, but don't worry; it doesn't last long.'

She was right, I thought, as I jiggled about in my seat. It was exactly like sitting on an ant's nest.

The drugs are on a timer and after each different concoction you have a flush out and so the whole procedure takes hours. As we were getting settled a pretty dark-haired young nurse came over and pulled up a chair. Her name was Laura, and she was the sister on the ward. We soon got talking; she was American and so her and my daughter chatted away about Dallas. Sarah had a flatmate from there and they'd become great friends, so much so that Sarah was thinking of going to live there for a few months. Laura told us about her life and how she had come to England many years ago, about her job as a chemotherapy nurse, her love of running and how when she had finished a shift she enjoyed nothing more than curling up on the couch with her kids and watching a good movie. She put us both at ease; it was like chatting to an old friend and I almost forgot I was being given toxic drugs through my veins.

After we'd had a sandwich and cup of tea another nurse came over with a box.

'This is for you,' she said, handing me a brown box that had ice-skating penguins on it with Christmas hats. 'It's from a charity called Chemo Hero,' she explained. 'They give out boxes of kindness to everyone going through chemotherapy.'

Tears sprang to Sarah's and my eyes as I opened the parcel. Inside the box were wet wipes, hand sanitizer, herbal tea, throat lozenges, mints, note book and pen, a tablet dispenser, an eyebrow shaper; all sorts of wonderful useful items. As Sarah and I looked through the gifts I found a card from Lisa Wallis, founder of chemo hero. The nurse came back, refilling my water jug.

'She must be a very special lady to have set up these boxes,' I said, still taking out items and examining them. The nurse explained that Lisa had been a young patient on the ward. She'd had breast cancer too and had set up the charity to help other people going through treatment.

The Herceptin was given as a drip into my vein that was administered over a couple of hours. The first infusion is the most important as, if you are going to, then you'll usually have a reaction on this first round and so you have your blood pressure and temperature taken at regular intervals and are asked to report any strange feelings immediately. So far so good: it seemed my body was absorbing the liquid without an issue.

'One down,' I said, looking at Sarah.

We left the ward at seven o'clock that evening. It had been a very long day and both of us were ready to be back at home.

'What did it feel like?' Terry asked.

'Nothing really, I mean you feel the needle when they put that in, then it's taped to your hand but you can't feel the liquid going into your veins, there's no burning or strange sensation, you can almost forget it's happening,' I told him. 'The worse bit is the ants in your pants from the steroids.'

I had been given a mountain of pills to take: more steroids and anti-sickness medication. I had been told the key is to take your anti-sickness before you need them, as if you're being sick then it's too late, as you won't be able to keep them down. *Makes sense*, I thought, as I dispensed my drugs into the plastic container that had been in my Chemo Hero box.

Chemotherapy is administered over several sessions (or cycles) of treatment spread over a few months. Each one takes 21 days (three weeks). On the first day of each cycle, you will be given your particular dose, as each batch is tailor made, taking into account your weight, and the drugs you are to be treated with. You will then have no chemotherapy for the next 20 days. At the end of the 21 days, you will start your second cycle. You will usually have between four and six cycles depending upon what your oncologist has advised.

You may get some of the side effects, but you are very unlikely to get all of them. Always tell your nurse about the side effects you have. Your doctor can prescribe drugs to help control some of these, especially sickness, and you will be given anti sickness drugs to be taken at home. It is very important to take the drugs exactly as your nurse has explained. This means they will more likely work better for you. It's easier to prevent sickness than to treat it. It's surprising how many people miss this vital information and don't take the preventive pills, because they don't feel sick - yet. Take them as prescribed; it will make you so much more comfortable.

Chemotherapy can reduce the number of white blood cells in your blood. This will make you more likely to get an infection, especially colds and flu. Your white blood cells start to reduce five to seven days after treatment and are usually at their lowest 10 to 14 days after. When the number of white blood cells is low, this is called neutropenia. This is the time to keep away from public places or high-risk infection areas like schools or large group meetings. Wash your hands and use sanitizer. Try to keep germs to a minimum.

If you start to feel unwell then don't hesitated to contact the hospital straight away on the contact number you've been given if:

- Your temperature goes over 38°C - make sure you buy a thermometer.

- You have symptoms of an infection – these can include feeling shaky, a sore throat, a cough, and severe diarrhoea.

- You are being sick and not able to keep anything down.

The number of white blood cells usually increases steadily and returns to normal before your next treatment. You'll have a blood test before having more chemotherapy. I always went to my doctor's surgery the day before my chemotherapy was due but I've heard of other ladies having their blood tests done on the same day at the chemo unit. If your white blood cells are still low, your doctor may delay your treatment for a short time until the count has gone back up again.

Anaemia (low number of red blood cells) can be another issue. Chemotherapy can reduce the number of red blood cells in your blood. These cells carry oxygen around the body. If the number of red blood cells is low, you may be tired and breathless. Tell your doctor or nurse if you feel like this. If you are very anaemic, you may need a drip to give you extra red blood cells (blood transfusion).

Your mouth may become sore and you may get ulcers. This can make you more likely to get an infection in your mouth. Gently clean your teeth morning and night and after meals. Use a soft-bristled toothbrush. It's important to follow any advice you are given and to drink plenty of fluids. It's a good idea to change your toothbrush after every cycle too, as this will help to prevent infections. I bought a supply of cheap children's toothbrushes and made sure I changed mine regularly. Again, don't suffer alone and tell your nurse if you have any problems with your mouth. They can prescribe medicines to prevent or treat mouth infections and reduce any soreness.

Try to eat small meals regularly. Don't worry if you don't eat much for a day or two. If your appetite doesn't improve after a few days, let your nurse know. They can give you advice on getting more calories and protein in your diet. You may get a bitter or metallic taste in your mouth, or find that food tastes different. This should go away when your treatment finishes. Try using herbs and spices (unless you have a sore mouth or ulcers) or strong-flavoured sauces to give your food more flavour. Sucking boiled sweets can sometimes help get rid of a bitter or metallic taste. Your nurse can give you more advice. My favourite things to eat were usually carb rich and stodgy, don't panic! Your eating habits will return to normal when chemo has finished. It's a bit like being pregnant in that you can crave some strange things. On the other hand, some foods and drinks – for me it was coffee – can turn your stomach. So eat when you feel hungry and don't worry too much about what you are eating, as long as you are getting some nutrients. And if you really can't face fresh fruit and veg there are some amazing detox protein juices out there full of the good stuff. I made a point of having a least one glass of these a day.

It is a normal and very common side effect to feel not just tired but completely wiped out at different times in your cycle. For me days 3 – 5 were the worst. It's often harder towards the end of treatment and for some weeks after it's finished, as there does seem to be a cumulative effect. Try to pace yourself and get as much rest as you need. Sleep when you need to; if you listen to your body it will tell you what it needs. Steroids can play havoc with your sleep patterns so it's important to get that rest when you can and not worry too much if, like me, you end up decorating at midnight or watching soaps at 2am. It's all normal and part of the chemo rollercoaster ride your body is on.

You usually lose all the hair on your head. This, to most people, is the most traumatic part of the whole process. Cut off our tits, fill us with toxic chemicals, but lose our hair and we are gibbering wrecks. So far you've been able to hide your cancer from the world; anyone passing you in the street or on the school run probably wouldn't have a clue of the treatment you have been going through. Now all of a sudden the world and his wife will know and pass judgement, give advice or delight you with tales of people they have known who have died from cancer. Believe me, if you thought people who are not medically trained could offer advice on your treatment before, it's now on a whole new level as it seems it's open season to patronize you, your doctors, and the life-saving treatment you are having, as there are a lot of people out there who just love to impart their wisdom.

My advice to you? Take it on the chin, thank them respectfully and move on. Their insensitivities are usually brought about by trying to help, so just let it go. You might want to chop a few names off next year's Christmas list though.

Along with your hair, your eyelashes, eyebrows and other body hair may also fall out. This usually starts after your first or second cycle of chemotherapy. It is almost always temporary and your hair will grow back after chemotherapy ends although sometimes - rarely - the hair loss is permanent. It is important to cover your head to protect your scalp when you are out in the sun until your hair grows back and in the winter get yourself a cosy sleep cap as bald heads in bed can get very chilly!

You will be entitled to an NHS wig and will be advised of how to apply for one. Believe me they are fantastic! I loved my wig and although it was sometimes impractical to wear it all the time, or simply too hot, I would say go for it and get one! The styles and colours on offer are amazing through the NHS and you are usually invited to a local salon who are used to dealing with patients. Don't be put off by horror stories; NHS wigs have changed! And you may find yourself only needing to wear it for a short time after all, so don't get wasting hundreds of pounds on a fancy wig that you may never wear – unless of course you're loaded – then buy as many as you like!

Nothing quite prepares you for losing your hair. It's the hardest blow and, for me, was the nadir of my cancer journey. I was bald, boobless, blown up from steroids and eating too many carbs, but it was only when I lost my hair that I really felt ugly and worthless. I wanted to have the old me back so badly; I ached for my former self. How had I come to this? Looking in the mirror was painful; I hated the reflection that was looking back at me. I hardly recognized myself. Luckily, my husband just carried on as normal and although I did catch a few pitying looks I felt he treated me much the same. The look on my father's face however, the first time he saw me without any hair, nearly broke my heart.

Nails may become brittle and split easily. They may get darker or discoloured with ridges on them. These changes usually grow out over several months after treatment finishes. Rarely, nails may come off, but they will grow back after treatment. Wearing gloves for washing up or using detergents will help protect your nails during treatment. Painting them with dark colours can help to reduce nail loss; don't forget your toenails!

You may get numb or tingling hands or feet. These symptoms are caused by the effect of chemotherapy on nerves. It's called peripheral neuropathy. You may also find it hard to fasten buttons or do other fiddly tasks and struggle to hold things.

Tell your doctor if you have these symptoms. They sometimes need to lower the dose of the drug. The symptoms usually improve slowly after treatment finishes, but in some people, they may never go away. Talk to your doctor if you are worried about this.

There are loads of less common side effects from chemotherapy that include:

Problems when going for a wee, as the drugs can irritate your bladder.

Eyes watering, or blurred vision. I couldn't see properly for a few days each cycle.

Soreness of feet or palms and nails. Try not to pick your nails as this can cause an infection. Remember to moisturize and avoid getting cuts and scratches. I was scratched by a cat and ended up with a nasty case of Cellulitis, which luckily was treated with an antibiotic. Cellulitis is dangerous and with a weak immune system you need to be vigilant and those caring for you need to be, too. It's a good idea for any carers to have a good idea of what to look out for, as if you do become unwell you may not be able to voice your concerns.

Most importantly do not suffer in silence. There is always someone who will be able to help you, so don't be afraid to ask.

Photo Diary

Waiting for my consultant. Just about to get my results and find out I need a mastectomy.

The week after my mastectomy, when my mum had washed my hair.

I had my hair cut short just before

starting chemotherapy.

Embracing new hats and scarves.

Amazingly my bald head was quite evenly shaped! I lost most of my hair by the second cycle.

My NHS wig! This is me on holiday, I enjoyed wearing my wig to go out in, although it did get hot and itchy.

It was good though, to be able to get dressed up and feel like the old me once in a while, even thought the first thing I did when I got home was to take it off and have a good scratch!

Back at work 3 months after finishing chemotherapy.

My breast care nurse organised a grant from Macmillan for me. I was so touched, I vowed to 'pay it back' by organising a fundraising event.

Another outing for my glamorous wig!

If you look very closely you can see my knitted knocker too!

8 months after finishing chemotherapy and my hair is growing back. Unfortunately it came back curly and grey!

First colour at 10 months post-chemo.

At last a few highlights and I'm starting to feel like me again!

Growing nicely! 12 months Post chemo. Just before going into hospital for my DIEP reconstruction.

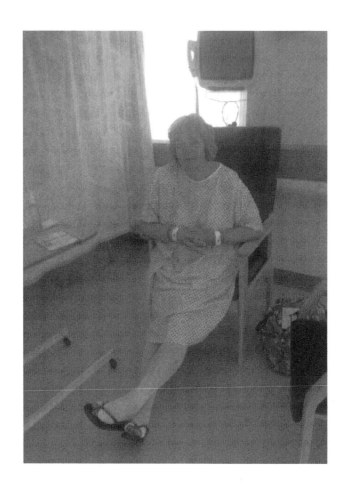

Final operation, reduction and uplift of my good boob.
Almost 2 years to the day of diagnosis.

After my last operation. DIEP on left breast and reduction on my right with dog ear revision on my abdomen scar.

I have to wait 6 months now for a nipple for my 'flap.'

Chapter Eight

* * *

The Chemo Diaries

These are the entries I made whilst on my first round of chemotherapy. The further three cycles took on a similar pattern; although after my first reaction to Docetaxel I was given Piriton intravenously and luckily never had the rash again.

Thursday 8th December
1st Night: Feeling surprisingly okay. I didn't know what to expect, but hadn't figured on feeling this good! Slight nausea, took Gaviscon. Felt better by 5.30 am. Woke up with blurry vision and an awful metallic taste in my mouth. Heartburn eased off when I got out of bed. Had an awful headache so took a couple of paracetamol and a cup of ginger tea. The ginger tea and biscuits are helping keep the nausea at bay. Making sure I keep up with my anti-sickness tablets.

2nd Day: Felt good amazingly, went for a walk, no nausea, kept up with my medication. Had a reasonable night. Read on the breast cancer forum to keep a banana by your bed and eat it before getting up in the morning as it helps with the sickness. Also, drink loads of water which I have been doing, as this helps to flush it out of your system. Not sure when the side effects are going to kick in as I'm managing pretty okay at the moment. It's not too bad, if it's all like this then I'll be fine!

3rd Day: All right in the morning, but by midday feeling much worse. After a heavy afternoon nap, I woke up to find it had arrived. Slept a lot, but not much nausea, drank loads of water and ginger tea, which helped. Really sensitive to noise, and grumpy; feeling very sorry for myself. Not been to the loo, so started on the laxatives.

4th Day: Very tired and emotional, kept crying and feel like shit. Awful night sweats. Sat in the bath just wanting it to be all over. Couldn't stop crying. Feel too knackered to stay positive. Had to get help to get me out of the bath, feel like a dead weight. I ache all over – feels like the worst case of flu and a bad hangover all rolled into one. Developed a rash on arms, inside thighs and buttocks. Looks like measles. Stayed in bed all day. Didn't want to see or speak to anyone. This is tough. I'm not sure I can do this.

5th Day: Skin now really bad, I rang the chemo ward, who said not chemo related probably just a rash. Ugh!! I know it's a bloody rash, it's driving me mad! Sat in the bath with porridge oats all over me, but that just made it worse so showered it off and covered myself with Sudocrem but that just made me itch more! Sent Terry out for calamine lotion: anything to try and sooth it.

Spoke to Sarah, she said I need to talk to Terry to address my fears about losing my hair. She said rash was probably just anxiety and if I talked to Terry then it would probably go away. I had a chat with him, told him I was scared and didn't want to be bald. He told me a chrysalis has to shed its coat to become a beautiful butterfly. God, I love that man. Rash still bloody here though!

6th Day: Had enough of the rash. I went to the pharmacy who told me to go to my GP. They were great at the surgery, fitted me in and I was given antihistamines and antibiotics. Said it looked like a Docetaxol rash. Bloody chemo! I knew it was an allergic reaction. Felt better instantly, got loads more energy. The steroids are keeping me pumped up; managed to paint the whole of the hallway and eventually got some sleep.

7Th Day: Up all night on steroid circus, watched TV and painted the coffee table. Still have mild nausea but craving stodgy food like cheese on toast, ginger biscuits, creamy tomato soup and pasta! Bit worn-out (well I was up most of the night) finding it hard to sleep and switch off but generally a lot better. Rash is subsiding, just got loads of tiny blisters all over, looks revolting.

8th Day: Everywhere is drying up - and I mean everywhere! Very sore down below, my mouth has an ulcer and my lips are peeling. Even my eyes hurt. My vision is still blurry and although I'm not sleeping I've got bags of energy. Using special mouthwash Sarah got me and a soft toothbrush that's helping with the skin peeling in my mouth. I'm still pigging out on carbs though; can't seem to stop eating. I thought you were supposed to lose weight on chemo? At this rate I'm gonna be the size of a house!

9th Day: Taste and appetite returning to normal, feel like I'm stabilizing and coming out of the chemo fog. My eyes are still streaming and my nose is dripping like a tap and I can smell EVERYTHING! Slept better and the rash has gone right down and not itching anymore – thank god. Went out for a lovely walk, even managed to concentrate and read for a while. It's been impossible to focus on the small words; my brain just couldn't cope with it! Watched a good film and had a laugh with Terry after dinner. First good laugh I've had in a while. Felt good to be getting back to normal.

*

Chemotherapy was every twenty-eight days and life swung into a pattern of good weeks and bad. Some cycles I had horrendous diarrhoea and others I simply couldn't go without laxatives. Each cycle got harder as the cumulative effect took its toll on my body and my mind. On the bad days, it felt like a whole rugby squad had beaten me up. Exhausted, drained and an emotional wreck, I could hardly see the point in getting out of bed. I just wanted to curl up in a ball, block out the world and die. Luckily this passed quickly enough and periods of sanity could be interspersed with these black days. I learnt to figure in treats even if it was a visit to the nail bar to get my nails painted with a gothic dark varnish in the vain hope that they wouldn't fall off, another charming side effect. By timing it right I could at least have a few normal weeks a month, and by keeping a diary, I could chart roughly where I would be in each cycle. It also had the added benefit of reminding me that it wouldn't last.

'Vaginal dryness happens due to a lack of oestrogen,' I said.

'Oh yeah?' was Terry's reply.

'Yeah I read it on the breast cancer forum, it's quite common,' I told him. Since having chemotherapy it had become almost impossible to have sex. My vagina was on fire. It felt like I was burning and I hadn't been the only one to notice.

'Breast cancer treatments can affect your hormones and make it difficult,' I carried on.

'You're telling me,' Terry added. 'You should get that woman to put condoms in her boxes of kindness.'

'Ha ha, I don't think it would always be appropriate, have you seen some of the old codgers on the ward?'

'All the more reason to enjoy themselves,' Terry said.

'They also said if you can bear with it, sexual intercourse actually helps as it stimulates the blood flow and helps keep it supple.'

'I like the sound of that, come to Dr Terry!' he said, grabbing hold of me.

'Alternatively, they said if it really is too painful try a vibrator or masturbating.'

'Where did you get this advice?' Terry wanted to know.

'On the Macmillan forum.'

'Wow, good old Macmillan! I must remember to pop a pound in their pot the next time I see one.'

'I also read in a book or somewhere that someone used lard as a lubricant.'

'Oh yeah, what about salted butter? We've got loads of that, or if you prefer olive oil, it's extra virgin...' Terry said cheekily.

'I was thinking of getting something from the chemist. The women on the forum recommend a product called Replens; they say you can get it free from your doctor. Next time I get a prescription I'll try and remember to ask for some. And no, I don't want a vibrator for Christmas before you ask!'

Cancer had become a big part of our lives. Like it or not, each day was peppered with the pink stuff. From hospital appointments for treatments, follow-ups with my oncologist and visits to Seamoor unit for either chemotherapy or Herceptin injections and with the blood test before each round, and heart scans, I was lucky to have a week without any appointments.

'I've had a date to go and order a wig next week,' I said, running my hand through my thinning hair that was somehow managing to hold on for dear life.

It was Christmas, I had my first chemo in early December and my next one wasn't due until New Year's Eve. I was going to feel relatively okay for Christmas Day I'd estimated, but New Year would be a write-off. My children had offered to come and cook our dinner and I was pleased to be able to let them take over. I was relieved to have them home, and more importantly, have a house full of joy and cheer. I needed the distraction and so did Terry.

On Boxing Day the kids left to visit their father. Exhausted, but pleased we had all been together, I sat down. My hair had been coming out by the handful over the last few days and I had been determined to keep it until after the Christmas dinner. As Sarah drove them both away in her car, I got Terry to fetch his shears.

'I want you to cut it all off,' I said tearfully, 'I can't stand it any longer. It's everywhere and it's upsetting me so much. Can you please just get rid of it for me?'

There is something surreal about your husband clipping off your hair. As I sat there with the machine whizzing past my ears I thought about the times I had seen Terry do this to his own head. I didn't want to be bald. I was dreading it. I had a line down my forehead that made me look like a Klingon and I always wore a fringe to hide it. There would be no hiding this; my wrinkles would be on show for the world to see.

'There all done,' he said gently, as I sobbed my heart out. The pain was awful; my beautiful long blond hair gone, thrown into the rubbish along with the Christmas wrapping paper. I took the hand mirror Terry was offering to me to inspect his work. Then, putting the mirror on the table, I hugged him as we both sobbed for what seemed like an age. This time it felt like cancer was winning. It had taken my breast, it had taken my sex life and now it had taken my crowning glory. How much lower could I go?

Chapter Nine

* * *

Bad News

The treatment was going well and, although it was unpleasant, I was coping. I had got used to having no hair and now wore my scarfs and hats with pride.

The look-good, feel-good charities know this is when you need that boost; this is when you need that kick up the backside to put some lipstick on! This is the one true time that makeup can make so much difference and I urge you to try to attend one of these inspirational events, as afterwards you really will feel so much better. As shallow as it sounds the two are inextricably linked: look good = feel better.

If you're too poorly to attend then this is a great opportunity for your nearest and dearest to spoil you and really make a difference. Get the makeup out and your scarfs have a bit of fun and try out new styles. I had a beautiful long blond wig courtesy of the NHS and was happy to wear it. I had chosen a wig that gave me the hair I'd always dreamed of having.

On our way to Exeter again and this time I was excited. We were off to see my plastic surgeon and hopefully, she would be able to give me a date for my reconstruction surgery.

'Won't they make you wait until you've finished your Herceptin injections?' Terry asked.

'I don't know,' I replied, 'I asked on the online forum and a few people said they wouldn't, but I can't imagine that they would do the op. I mean, the drug affects your heart and it's pretty powerful so I think she will prefer me to be off it. I really do want to get this over and done with! I'm so fed up of waiting - it's driving me crazy - but I have an awful feeling she's going to make me wait.'

'You are an ideal candidate for the DIEP breast reconstruction surgery,' my surgeon told me. As I was now six months smoke-free I was confident of a good outcome.

'There's just one problem; your BMI is too high. It's shot up and I need it to come down to do the operation. You have to lose weight,' she said, searching for her calculator. 'Ten kilos.'

'Okay,' I said, crestfallen, 'I can do that.'

'I won't be able to schedule your operation until you've lost it however.'

This wasn't what I wanted to hear.

'When you've reached the target,' she said, underlining the ideal weight I should be on a piece of paper, 'give my secretary a call and she'll pop you on the list,' she finished off, handing me a business card and circling her secretary's number.

'So they've got me to give up smoking and now I need to lose over a stone, what else will they want me to do? Jump through a hoop?' I asked Terry sarcastically as we trudged back to the car.

'Well, she wants you to have genetic testing too, didn't you hear that bit?' Terry asked.

'Oh god, at this rate I'm never going to have a new boob,' I wailed.

'She said you're an ideal candidate - you've just got to shift a few pounds first. Come on lardy arse, get yourself in the car.'

It was true, all the carb comfort eating I had been doing whilst going through chemo had caught up with me. I had piled on the pounds and hadn't given a thought to my expanding waistline. My diet had been the last thing on my mind.

'And anyway,' I said, 'they told me at the hospital the last thing they wanted was for me to lose weight; they actively encouraged me to eat what I felt like.'

'Yeah, but doughnuts for breakfast and pasta and chips for tea isn't a brilliant diet, Kaz.'

I felt wretched. I had scuppered my chances of reconstruction by being too fat for the operation. The joy and elation I had felt earlier that day had melted away and I settled back in the passenger seat in a grumpy mood.

'Let's get back to work; we always lose weight at the beginning of the season. You've nearly finished your chemo and it will do us both good,' Terry said, fastening his seat belt.

Later that day I phoned HR and asked if they had any short contracts available. We had had to decline our original works contract as we were due to start before my chemo ended and, with the best will in the world, there was no way I was going to be able to work on a campsite and live in a caravan whilst going through treatment.

It was good news. There were three contracts available: one for Devizes, one for Scarborough and one for Woodhall Spa.

'Lets go to Woodhall Spa, Terry.'

'Where is it? I've never heard of it,' he said, getting the map out to have a look.

'It's in Lincolnshire. It sounds nice, and it's not too far away from my mum and dad, so we would be able to visit them.' I hadn't seen my parents for ages as I was too ill to travel and they found it equally difficult to come all the way from Leicestershire to Devon.

It was settled with HR; we had a contract to start work in two months' time. Starting on the first of May, the contract ran until the twentieth of September; enough time to earn some money and, most importantly, get fit and lose weight.

I asked on the forum if anyone had any experience of the oncology department at Lincoln Hospital and a couple of ladies who lived in the area responded. Claire and Beverley gave me all the information I needed and, armed with the oncologist's name, I was able to phone his secretary and arrange to temporarily transfer my treatment.

My new oncologist's secretary was amazing and phoned me a few times just to make sure they had all the relevant information. I told my doctor in Barnstaple, at one of my regular check-ups, and after supplying the admin team with all the details of my new doctor in Lincoln they were able to liaise and share my records. We were ready to go off to work.

'What about a quick holiday?' I asked.
'Okay, but cheap - and let's go somewhere we know to make it easy, just in case you take poorly or anything. What about Greece?'

I got on to the Internet and found a bargain package holiday. Seven nights self-catering; just what I needed - a bit of total relaxation to set me up before I went back to work. I wasn't looking forward to going back - I still had no hair and with my uniform on I knew I was going to look like a bloke - but I didn't have much choice. The bills weren't going to get paid by me sitting around watching daytime TV and my bum certainly wouldn't be getting any smaller if we stayed at home.

The holiday did the trick. My aqua-knocker had been very useful. You couldn't tell that I was boobless and I had a great time sunbathing - not too much – swimming and getting my energy levels up ready for work. Back home, refreshed and relaxed, we set off with our caravan for our new base in Lincolnshire.

'I'm not going to get stressed. I'll do my core jobs, but I'm not killing myself. This year I'm going to enjoy working for the club,' I told Terry.

I had a final appointment with my oncologist at Barnstaple hospital and as Terry was busy I decided I would go on my own; after all, it was only a routine check-up. As I sat there with my oncologist opposite me, my file open on her consulting room table she asked how I'd been, and I told her about our holiday and going back to work.

'As you're at the end of your chemo now we need to schedule in radiotherapy,' she said. 'You'll need to go every day for two weeks and it's at Exeter, so if you start next week...'

'Stop,' I said, holding my hand up and with big fat tears trying to squeeze out of my eyes. 'I think you've got it wrong.'

Looking at me as if I was deranged, or was still suffering from my messed up chemo brain, she started to speak again. 'Yes, radiotherapy, you'll need to get there every day, there's a bus that goes from here to Exeter, but you have to wait around for the other passengers.'

My mind was whirring and the tears started to make an appearance.

'I don't think... I didn't think,' I corrected, 'that I needed radiotherapy. No-one ever said that. No-one mentioned radiotherapy.' I squeezed my eyelids shut to stop the tears from escaping. 'Can you just check? Can you please look in my file? I'm pretty sure I don't need radiotherapy.' There! I'd said it, stuck up for myself and questioned her judgement. *God, I wished Terry were here*, I thought.

Flicking through the pages in my hospital file, she traced her finger over my notes exclaiming, 'Oh no, that's right - you don't need radiotherapy.'

Back at work and luckily my manager also wanted to lose weight.

We joined Weight Watchers and my auntie gave me a bike, so Terry and I cycled everywhere. The club had changed our working hours so we no longer had to start at seven in the morning and work until eleven at night, we now started at a very reasonable nine o'clock and finished at eight o'clock when we were on the late shift and five thirty when we were on earlies. With two full days off in the week, the job had become so much easier than in previous years.

The site was beautiful and the customers in the main part behaved themselves. Our managers were a delight to work for and, even after driving them mad with all the day changes to accommodate my treatment, they remained friendly and calm. I'm sure their manner had a lot to do with my recovery. I don't think I could have put up with the selfishness of some of the managers I have worked for and would have probably blown my top if they had moaned about my constant hospital appointments. I never took a day off and managed to rearrange my days off so that I could attend my various hospital meetings without ever missing a day's work.

The thing you don't know when you first start out on this journey is just how many appointments you will have. Being diagnosed Her2 positive, I had heart scans every three months, and as I wasn't coping with my tablets and had awful carpal tunnel syndrome, I was back and forward see my oncologist almost every other week. I had to have genetic counselling too which, although I had seen a counsellor in Devon, Lincoln hospital insisted on repeating, despite me protesting that it was a waste of NHS money. I also had my first year follow-up, my annual mammogram and the appointment for the results. Every test, every scan, is proceeded by an appointment and boy do these appointments mount up! Suddenly we knew our way around Lincoln hospital nearly as well as Exeter and Barnstaple.

After a couple of months working on the site, we decided it would be nice to soak our bones in a well-needed bath and, with Devon being so far away, booked into a hotel in Skegness for the night.

'They say you can cycle all the way to Mablethorpe from Skegness,' I said shortly after we had left the hotel on the first morning for a bike ride. Eight hours later we reached the hotel that we had left behind at ten o'clock that morning. We had made it all the way to Mablethorpe, stopping off for sardines and a glass of chilled rosé at the Fat Seagull in Sutton on Sea on the way back.

'The sole has fallen off my shoe,' I laughed as I readjusted the towel I was now using to make my seat more comfortable.

'I'm not surprised! We've cycled miles Kaz; you've done really well. I'm so proud of you,' Terry said, loading my bike into our vehicle.

'I think I've well and truly earned that bath,' I said, hobbling up the ornate staircase to our room. I may have felt stiff, but my fitness had returned, chemo seemed a long time ago and my hair had started sprouting little tufts of fluff.

The Lincolnshire health authority, unlike Devon, has health care at home so at least I didn't have to go to the hospital every twenty-one days. A nurse comes to your house or, in my case, caravan. They phone the night before to confirm what time they will be with you and when they come they go through all the safety checks and administer the injection. They then have to wait with you for two hours just in case of a bad reaction, which could be anything from passing out to a full-blown heart attack. I was told it is usually a case of giving you a whiff of air, as fainting seems to be the most common side effect of the Herceptin injections. They then book you in for twenty-one days' time and after completing the paperwork are on their way. You're advised to sit and have a cup of tea and rest for half an hour but after that, you can carry on with light duties. It was so much simpler than having to go to hospital and as each time you had a wonderful nurse to chat with for a couple of hours it was fun too. I looked forward to having my treatments as I crossed them off the calendar.

Chapter Ten

* * *

Going All Out

Before we knew it our contract had finished and we were on our way home to Devon, fitter and healthier. I had a smattering of hair, and with money in our savings account again, we were buoyant and looking forward to a rest.

I was still having Herceptin injections and with the help of the lovely Sandra, my oncologist's secretary in Lincolnshire, I was transferred back to Barnstaple again. Devon didn't have health care at home and so I returned to traipsing back and forward to the hospital again. I was, however, nearing the finish line. My last injection, if everything went well, would be in December.

Back at home in Devon I excitedly searched through my purse to find the business card that my surgeon had given me in March.

'Hi,' I said introducing myself, 'I was told to call you as soon as I'd lost the weight, and had the results back from my genetic testing. I don't carry the Braca gene so I won't be requiring an Angelina Jolie I'm happy to report!' I joked. 'Can I be put on the list for reconstruction surgery now please?' There was an intake of breath on the other end of the line.

'You'll need to come and see your plastic surgeon before she can put you on the list.'

'Fantastic,' I said eagerly, getting my pen ready to put the date on my calendar.

'I will send you an appointment in the post.'

'Okay, when are we looking at? My husband and I are now back in Devon as we've finished work, so I'm free anytime.'

'Oh, I'm sorry - at the moment we're looking at December at the earliest to see her. She's very busy.'

I didn't doubt she was very busy what I did doubt was my chance of having my reconstruction surgery anytime soon. Disappointed, I put the phone down.

'At this rate, I'll still be waiting this time next year for the bloody operation,' I complained to Terry, frustrated. 'Do you think I should have just had implants?'

'No; you've done really well, lost the weight and as she said it's the gold star of breast reconstruction, no hard lumps or leaking silicone, having to have them changed in ten years. It's what you've been working for, just make sure they know you're ready for it and keep on at them.'

Terry was right. I had been sold on the DIEP reconstruction from the first time I had been told about it. They would take fat from my belly and with microsurgery transfer it to my chest wall making me a new breast. It would be my flesh, warm to the touch, wobble when I wobbled and, importantly, age with me.

'The secretary also said that there's an evening in November. It's for women contemplating breast surgery to go and meet women who have had it. She's going to put an invite in the post for me. She said patients found it really useful in making up their minds about which procedure to go with and you can see what the results look like,' I said. 'I'll ask Sarah if she wants to come with me. And in the meantime, we might as well go on holiday. I've found a really good bargain on the internet - why don't we have a break as it looks like it's going to be a while until I have my op and, let's face it, we've worked really hard this summer.'

I didn't really need to twist Terry's arm too much. I pulled up the holiday on the computer and with few clicks was ready to book us a fortnight in the sun, managing to fit it around my hospital appointments. I just needed the chemo ward to agree to postpone my Herceptin injection by five days.

'I'd better just check its ok to delay my Herceptin. Either that or bring the next one forward,' I told Terry.

After a chat with the receptionist and ward sister, it was agreed I could delay my Herceptin by five days. It was impossible to bring it forward as a minimum of twenty-one days' interval is required between treatments to prevent excess strain on the heart. A week's delay was acceptable; any longer and I would have to be reloaded again which would mean having to be monitored for six hours as I had been for my first injection.

'So we can go,' I said, as I put in my card details and pressed confirm. Two weeks away would be perfect. The last few months had been full of hospital appointments and we both really needed some normal time away without the word cancer rearing its ugly head every five minutes.

I phoned my mum to tell her.

'It's really reasonable for two weeks in Greece. It's probably a bit rough but hey ho, it's a holiday. It's not like we can afford anything else, not if we want to get through the winter on our savings. No fancy five-star hotels in the Caribbean this year, bloody cancer has a lot to answer for.'

It appeared my mum and dad had been to the resort we had booked and not only that had stayed at the same apartments! The holiday turned out to be the best medicine for both of us. We came back refreshed and ready to tackle the next part of my journey. I ticked off the weeks on my calendar until the day arrived when I would see my plastic surgeon.

In her office, she explained the surgery and introduced me to my specialist breast reconstruction nurse. I told her I had been to the show-and-tell evening, accompanied by my daughter Sarah, and met a couple of wonderful ladies. The ladies had answered our questions and had bravely shown us the results and their scars and sung the praises of the DIEP procedure. I had been blown away; the results were so natural and the ladies were more than happy with the outcome.

'So realistically, when do you think I can have my operation?' I asked.

She wouldn't be pinned down, so I guessed, 'April? May? June?' Her face told me the latter was more likely.

'June, you're kidding me? Six months time!' I cried, as the tears started to well up inside me. 'I can't wait that long, what am I supposed to do? Go back to work in March only to finish in June?'

My surgeon explained that there were a lot of ladies on her waiting list and as she only did two DIEP flap operations a month she had quite a list. I couldn't help thinking, *but I should have been put on that list months ago.* It had been last March when I first saw her and stupidly I had thought that as soon as I phoned to say I was ready and had lost the required weight I would have been added to the list. I was seething but trying to keep it all under control.

'I've finished work for this. I could have taken a longer contract but I was hoping I would have my reconstruction a lot sooner.'

'I'm sorry, but my diary is already quite full,' she said, flicking through my notes.

'But I've given up smoking, lost ten kilos, been tested for the Braca gene, I've even given up caffeine,' I pleaded, to no avail.

As we were getting up to leave I added, 'And I've stopped taking my Tamoxifen. My oncologist said I could have a break as I've been having really bad side effects.'

She asked me how long I had been off the drug and made a note of that before we shook hands and said goodbye. She would send me an appointment as soon as she could schedule me in but realistically we were looking at the summer.

Walking to the car in the rain, Terry and I were feeling decidedly downbeat.

'Well, I tried everything,' I complained. 'I'm just so annoyed this is going to take forever at this rate. It's doing my bloody head in. I'm so fed up with having to put our lives on hold. This stupid breast cancer has taken over and I just want an end to it.'

My phone had been switched off since entering the hospital but as we reached the car it pinged and I saw I had a voicemail message. It was my surgeon. She'd had a look at her diary and it turned out the lady she had in mind for January wouldn't be ready. She told me not to start retaking my Tamoxifen as she just might have a space for me.

'Oh my good god,' I cried, 'it worked! We threw everything at it and pushed it through. Thank god I told her I'd stopped taking my medication, I think that must have swung it,' I said excitedly.

'No, I think it was giving up tea and coffee that really impressed her the most,' Terry teased.

Chapter Eleven

* * *

Get Busy Living

My last Herceptin injection was quite emotional. As I walked onto the ward, I held out a large box of chocolates and thank you card. I scanned the room filled with people hooked up to the machines receiving their life-saving or in some cases palliative treatments. Some looked like old hats at it, while a few looked nervously around the room, just starting their journey. Week in, week out, seven days a week with no respite for holidays, the room would be full of people like me who had received the devastating diagnosis that everyone dreads to hear, 'I'm sorry you have cancer.'

In the months after finishing work and waiting for my next adventure, (my DIEP reconstruction had been scheduled for January 30th) I'd had time to reflect. I had been so busy with finishing chemo and then going off to work and living in a different county, I hadn't had a chance to contemplate what I had been through. Post traumatic shock syndrome was a long way from knocking on my door, but slight worries and what if's had been tapping on my windows. I'd had time on my hands again, and you know what that does. My little devil was rearing its scary little head. Perhaps I had been spending too much time on the online forums, or as Terry put it, hanging about with people who inevitably weren't going to make it. In my 'normal' non-cancer world I simply would never have come into contact with these brave souls, many of who were fighting for their lives.

I read reports and research papers that I found online. I scared myself half to death with survival statistics. I read biographies of famous people who had fought and lost their cancer battle. It all made rather grim reading. And then there were the films that depicted breast cancer, where the protagonist never survived, it seemed that cancer was all around me, and with so many unhappy endings.

You can get busy living, or get busy dying - I had chosen life a long time ago, now I just had to remember how to live it and get that pesky little demon off my back. I turned to my pink sisters online and it seemed I wasn't alone; it was easy to slip over to the dark side and start the imagination free-falling into an abyss of what ifs.

'You have to live life like you're going to live, not like you're going to die – because after all, we're all going to die one day,' one inspirational lady advised. She was right but it didn't stop me from reading everything I could lay my hands on about survival rates and statistics.

Survival for all stages of breast cancer:

Generally, for women with breast cancer in England and Wales, ninety-five percent will survive for one year after diagnosis.

Almost 90 out of every 100 women (almost 90%) will survive their cancer for 5 years or more after diagnosis.

Almost 80 out of every 100 women (almost 80%) will survive their cancer for 10 years or more after diagnosis.

Around 65 out of every 100 women (around 65%) are expected to survive their cancer for more than 20 years after diagnosis.

Survival by stage:

No UK-wide statistics are available for different stages of breast cancer or individual treatments. These statistics are from one area of England for people diagnosed between 2002 and 2006.

Stage 1: Most women (around 99%) will survive their cancer for 5 years or more after diagnosis.

Stage 2: Almost 90 out of 100 women (almost 90%) will survive their cancer for 5 years or more after diagnosis.

Stage 3: Almost 60 out of 100 women (almost 60%) will survive their cancer for 5 years or more after diagnosis.

Stage 4: 15 out of 100 women (15%) will survive their cancer for 5 years or more after they are diagnosed. The cancer is not curable at this point, but may be controlled with treatment for some years.

I read the information but really was none the wiser. I had read accounts of women being diagnosed with Grade Two cancers with no lymph node involvement that had had their cancer come back, metastasising in their bones, liver or brain, to now be deemed treatable, but not curable. The more research I did the more I realised it was a lottery. There just didn't appear to be any correlation between the type of cancer patient and the risk of the disease returning.

I carried on with my research, determined to find out more. I had read about taking turmeric and upping my vitamin D levels, even treating with cannabis oil, but I still didn't know the cause, or what my risk of it coming back actually was. I knew breast cancer was one of the most common cancers in the UK. Staggeringly, one in eight women would succumb to it in their lifetimes. As I read the list I couldn't help wondering if all these crazy women dressed up in pink running races for life or getting muddy were onto something. It appeared the fitter you are, the less likely the cancer will return; perhaps it was time to dust off my trainers and start running.

It's no wonder that one of the most common fears (that old friend again) for people diagnosed with cancer is, what happens if it returns? Cancer can come back if any of the cancer cells are left behind after treatment and there is no way of knowing this until they rear their ugly heads again. This could be anything from a year to thirty years down the line; the truth is once you have had breast cancer you are on watch. You have to patrol your body vigilantly for signs of a recurrence and hope you will spot the signs. Sometimes a mammogram will pick it up early or, more commonly, it won't be until the cancer is large enough to be detected as a lump that you find when you're checking your breasts.

Local recurrence is when the cancer occurs in the same spot again.

Regional recurrence means the cancer has grown in the tissues or lymph nodes around the original cancer area.

Distant recurrence is when the cancer has spread to an area far away from the original location of the cancer. When this occurs, health care providers say the cancer has metastasized.

I slowly came to realize that there is nothing you can do to make sure your cancer will not return, but there are some steps you can take to try to stay as upbeat and healthy as possible:

Eat healthy foods. There is no proof that eating healthy foods will prevent your cancer from coming back, but it may improve your overall health. And there is some evidence that a diet rich in fruits and vegetables and low in saturated fats may help reduce the risk of recurrence of some types of cancers.

Limit alcohol use. Some cancers are linked to drinking alcohol.

Get regular exercise. Exercise can help improve your overall health, boost your mood, and help you stay at a healthy weight.

Most importantly, try not to let your fears get the best of you. Kick that little demon into touch. Focus on being as healthy as possible. Get back to your daily routine. Focus on the little things that make you happy, whether it is having dinner with a friend, playing with your grandchildren, or walking with your dog. Smack that anxiety out of the window and try, as hard as it may seem, to put it all behind you.

There is help out there for anyone struggling. Macmillan offer an amazing website full of help and also man a switchboard to help with any concerns you or your loved ones may have about cancer. I know my daughter found them particularly helpful when after Googling Her2 breast cancer she had scared herself half witless and had convinced herself that I was about to die. She confided in me much later on that, when she didn't know where to turn, Macmillan were there for her.

Do a search for cancer centres in your local area and you should be able to find places that you can turn to for help. Maggie's centres, Haven, and Penny Bhron to name a few. They all have dedicated counsellors and are there for you.

Many ladies have told me that mindfulness worked for them, or yoga, or simply joining a breast buddies club to meet up with like-minded women who have been there and got the t-shirt. Sometimes it's by only spending time with others that have been through the same trauma that we can find true peace. Sadly, once you've been diagnosed and have joined the pink ladies, it's the one club that you never quite leave.

Chapter Twelve

* * *

The DIEP Diaries

I had my pre-operative meeting the week before and now at 6:45 on a frosty January morning, Terry and I were walking the empty corridors to the admissions ward. Dragging my suitcase behind me, I was excited and nervous at the same time. I had hardly slept. The day I had been waiting for had arrived. Sixteen months after I had said goodbye to my breast, I was about to have my new one sewn onto me.

The twelve-hour operation with two teams of plastic surgeons was imminent and I couldn't stop myself from continually nipping to the toilet for a nervous wee. I didn't have to wait long as the teams of anaesthetist surgeons and nurses all did their bit. Blood was taken, my blood pressure monitored. My white blood cell count had been low the week before, and after repeated tests at my doctor's surgery, I was deemed fit for the operation. I had picked up an awful cold at Christmas and was only just getting rid of it proving that, although nine months ago, the chemotherapy that had wrecked my immune system was making it hard to shake off a simple cold. I knew my surgery and recovery were going to be arduous and had been doing everything in my power to prepare for it. I was swimming three times a week, going for long walks and with Salsa dancing once a week I felt fit and ready.

Nothing, however, could have prepared me for the way I would feel after my surgery.

These are extracts from my diary.

1st Day: Out of surgery and I'm in a private room. I can't move. I'm on a bed with cannulas and wires everywhere. I don't need to worry about going to the loo, I have a tube for that. I have an oxygen mask, so I barely have to breathe. There is a machine inflating and deflating enormous cricket pads that are strapped tightly to my shins, pumping air in and out like a giant breath. I have a plastic lilo on my torso that is hot, so hot the sweat is pouring down my forehead and stinging my eyes. It's to keep me warm, I'm told. This is my bear hugger. My new flap must be kept warm. The survival of it depends on the blood supply and keeping me boiling hot will encourage the blood to supply the delicate tissue so that it doesn't die. I can't see it - I have bandages all over - even if I could lift my head, which I can't. I lie here like a coma patient, all I can do is see, hear, smell and breathe. I have no idea why I have put myself through this. I feel helpless and afraid.

2nd Day: Every twenty minutes, day and night, the nurses come into my room. I have a blood pressure monitor strapped to my right arm so they don't need to keep applying one. But they poke and prod me. They have to listen to my flap to make sure the blood is pumping. They use a Doppler and it picks up the beat of the blood flowing, they have to put it on two sites and to make their job easier they have drawn on me with felt tip pen where to place the machine.

As soon as they are satisfied that my flap is alive and warm I'm left alone again to drift in and out of sleep along to the buzzing and bleeping of the machines attached to me. I can see a computer screen to my right hand on a trolley that is whirring, the wires snaking under my bedclothes attached to my skin. I remember I'm being monitored, Cynthia is conducting her research project, and these are her probes gathering data on the flashing screen. I have a morphine pump and with the slightest squeeze my pain is controlled, they feed me other medicine too. I'm not sure what it is but I get injected in my stomach on a regular basis. They turn me and check for sores. I'm told I have a sore patch on my heel from being in the same position for over twelve hours in surgery and a plastic cushion is found for my creamed foot. I have four tubes attached to drain bottles all filling with liquids. Two are in my chest area, and one either side of my abdomen. The cannula that has been drip-feeding me a saline solution is removed and they bring me drinks. I manage with a straw and later that day I eat for the first time. A watery soup I think, but I can't be sure.

At night all hell breaks loose. The night nurse checking my Doppler discovers I'm losing blood. I hadn't noticed. It's soaked my sheets, soaked my hospital gown. She cleans me up and redresses the dressings but it isn't good. My flap is going black, the colour is draining from it and it's starting to die. I'm in their hands as I can't do a thing to help myself.

3rd Day: My surgeon has been to see me again, she's not happy with my flap. The necrosis has started and in order to give my flap the best chance, she needs to trim part of it off. A simple, four-hour operation, which she plans to do tomorrow – unless it becomes any worse. She explains it's nothing to worry about and I have a good big flap so losing a bit on the side where it wasn't supporting itself won't decrease the size much. It turns out the other plastic surgeon, who happened to be a man, had tried to make my flap as big as possible, but sadly it wasn't to be.

'Typical man,' I say, 'always wanting bigger boobs.'

I can move more now. I'm encouraged to get out of bed and sit in the chair. The pain is unbearable though, even with my morphine friend. The nurses show me how to swing my legs and lever myself up but I don't like it and get back into bed. I can't imagine ever getting out of the crisp white sheets. I can't imagine ever being able to walk again.

4th Day: I ask if I can sign my consent form for my operation with a cross, as I can't even manage my signature. I feel ill. I feel the necrosis in my breast is poisoning me and can't wait to get into theatre to have the dying flesh removed.

Back in my room I'm drugged up and sleeping. I tell Terry to have the day off from visiting me. I'm so out of it and all I want is sleep. My surgeon visits. It all went well; they trimmed it off. My original flap was one and a half kilos, she tells me, so I still have an ample sized new breast. I manage a weak smile and thank her. I'm so doped up I'm not even bothered about looking. All I crave is sleep and morphine. The lights are dimmed and I'm left alone. I can't sleep though and the computer monitor is restless too, making so much noise with the cooling fan and its bleeps. Cynthia has already told me if at any time I felt uncomfortable or that the machine was intrusive, I could opt out of the research project. I've had enough. I press my call bell and ask for it to be removed. I am boiling hot, sleep deprived, tetchy and can take no more. I hope I have done enough for them to gather their information but I need to rest.

5th Day: My catheter is being removed so I will have to walk; luckily I have my own bathroom. They bring a commode in; even they think making it to my bathroom would be a step too far. I make the commode with help from Terry, he's been here nearly every day, making the three-hour round trip to be at my side. As he leans in to help me I smell him, he smells of coffee and almonds, he smells of aftershave and home. I want to nuzzle into him, not letting go, and be transported out of the stifling hot room.

I fart. I fart for what seems like eternity and I catch the young nurse trying hard not laugh, biting her top lip trying to keep a straight face as I apologize for the procrastinated sound. My bowels aren't moving yet, despite the copious amounts of laxatives I am being given. I fear if I pass wind again I will pebble dash my bed and so reluctantly I leave the comfort of the commode with little more than hot air for all my efforts and swing my legs one at a time, breathing through the pain, back into my hot house bed. I still have to have the magic pumping boots on and the red-hot blanket. I do at least get a bed bath and get to keep my cold flannel pressed to my temples. The nurse soothes my brow and freshens my sheets and pillows. I am being so well looked after and, so far, there is no sign of Nasty Nurse. I feel better in myself, the relief of being out of the bear hugger and the heat! I never thought I would be able get out of bed again.

6th Day: I'm a lot livelier today. I think the skin necrosis had made me feel quite rough and today, pumped full of antibiotics and heavy drugs, I feel so much better. I get out of bed, make it to my bathroom and even, amazingly, go to the loo. After six days with no movement it feels like heaven on earth. A young nurse gets me into my chair and, fetching a bowl of water and taking off my surgical stockings, washes my feet. I'm still in the hospital gown and unable to do much more than lift a cup and eat my meals. But the boots and the heated blanket have been removed. My tummy is pulling and the only way I can move around is bent over double.

I have a visitor, my original surgeon who performed my mastectomy, comes to see me. She heard I was on the ward. She looks like an angel, with her blond shiny hair and it takes a few moments for me to register who she is.

A nurse asks if I wouldn't mind moving onto the ward now and I agree. I have a new bed by the window with fresh air to breathe. After being cooped up in the tiny room for so long it feels wonderful. I have company too; an old lady opposite me who is a real chatterbox. She's had a biopsy for breast cancer. She doesn't know if she has it yet but the biopsies have bruised her breast tissue badly and as she lives alone and is inclined to pass out they have decided to keep her in. There's a retired headmistress next to her. She had her appendix out in the night and is drifting in and out of sleep, her snores punctuated by the odd fart here and there. Then at the end of the ward is a lady with her eyes bandaged up. I have no idea what that's all about.

I think there was an ulterior motive in moving me out of my room, as I now have to walk miles to the toilet clutching my cough pillow to my abdomen. I hobble, hunched over, one step at a time as the old lady races past me with her walking frame. Everywhere hurts but my abdomen is the most painful. Even the effort of flushing the toilet causes me to wince and if I'm not careful a slight turn can floor me. I can't imagine getting out of here, I feel so tired and worn out, all I want to do is rest.

7th Day: It's noisier on the ward and I'm thankful I've got my headphones and audio books. Old Mrs Chatterbox hasn't stopped the whole time I've been in here, with only a short respite for sleep. Luckily the headmistress is awake now and so she can interrogate her. I can listen to my book and zone out. I feel much brighter today and have even started to make an effort with my appearance. I used my dry shampoo and brushed my hair for the first time in days. I even made it to the bathroom with my cough pillow, toothpaste and toothbrush and cleaned my teeth. I thought I could have managed a strip wash but I was only able to rinse the cooling flannel and wash my hands and face.

The physiotherapist came today and made me do some exercises. She was a little sheepish as the last time she had come I told her she was mad and to go away. She seemed pleased I was, at last, making an effort. I asked her if she had ever had major abdominal surgery. She hadn't. 'Well if you had,' I told her, 'you would know it feels as if you've been run over by a truck - and not just one of those little lorries, a great big twin-wheeled articulated one. And just as you feel you can get up it reverses back over you.' She smiled and said, 'Point taken. But we need to get you walking up stairs before you go home tomorrow.'

The thought of my stairs at home fills me with dread, I know I need to get up them but god knows how that is going to happen.

8th Day: My super surgeon has given me a reprieve. I don't have to go home today. She said that, as I'd had further surgery, I am a few days behind in my recovery and so it would be better if I stayed in the hospital for another day at least. She is on call and if anything goes wrong it's better that I'm here and not an hour and a half away. I'm happy to stay. I'm frightened to leave the safety of the hospital. I've only been in a week but I can't imagine fending for myself ever again in the big wide world. I still have three drains and I'm carrying them around like precious pets.

9th Day: Things move on fast and every day I'm improving drastically. I had my stair assessment, which I did easily, to the delight of the young physiotherapist. I didn't even give her any lip. She went away smiling and declared me fit for discharge. I'm ready to go home too. The ward has become even busier. Mrs Chatterbox is still lingering, the headmistress is in so much pain she is convinced they have left a swab or a scalpel inside her and the blind lady had a stream of noisy visitors. We now have another patient, too. A lady came in early yesterday evening after being bitten by her cat. I saw her mangled hand as I hobbled by on my way to the bathroom. Her pet moggy had sunk its teeth into her flesh, ripping through the skin, and infection had set in. She was scheduled to go into theatre later last night. This morning I heard the doctor telling her that it hadn't been successful and that the bacteria was deep rooted - so much so they needed to go in again and see if they could clean it out but that she should be prepared for the worst - she might end up losing her hand! The poor woman she said she'd had the bloody cat for sixteen years and this is how it repays her!

Terry came after lunch and loaded me into a wheel chair. He forgot my coat and boots so he wrapped me up in my dressing gown and at last, piled with cushions on all sides and my heart pillow under my seat belt, we headed home.

Chapter Thirteen

* * *

More Rest and Recovery

I was the perfect patient and, just as I had promised my surgeon I would, I did everything by the book. She had terrified me before I left and told me how one of her patients had taken her bra off, swung round and her flap had fallen off, and this was three weeks after surgery. I was not to do anything but rest and I wasn't allowed to lift anything heavier than a half-full kettle. I assured her that I hadn't waited all this time to mess it up by doing unnecessary housework. I wouldn't be touching the hoover for a very long time.

'If your flap goes cold or starts to look black then its 999, no messing about; in an ambulance and straight into emergency theatre,' she told me. 'It's that serious; any delay could result in a total flap failure.'

I got the picture and assured her that between Terry and I we would guard my breast like a newborn baby.

We swung into a happy rhythm, the day only being punctuated by the visit from the district nurse to change my bandages and empty my drains. They oohed and aahed, never having seen the microsurgery before, and I felt privileged to have been offered the reconstruction. We kept to our word and my new boob was frequently handled to test the temperature and make sure the colour was good. I was still pretty weak and after a trip to the bathroom, a strip wash and change of bra, I was back in bed for the first week at home as this is all that I could manage. I had to wear a bra day and night for six weeks; so every day I changed into a freshly laundered one and this simple act made it more bearable. It was going to be a long road to recovery but so far the results were amazing. I was thrilled with my new breast and pleased I had endured the harrowing surgery.

It can take 12- 16 weeks to recover from DIEP reconstruction surgery. It's a good idea to wear support knickers or an abdominal belt for a few weeks too until the swelling has gone down. Don't forget you have had surgery on two sites and with multiple incisions it may take you quite some time to get back to normal. My surgeon told me to allow at least a year to fully recover, as it's important to take the time to heal and heal well. This is one of those times when you really do need to do as you are told!

As I admired my new 'foob' in the long length mirror I was happy with the results. The surgery had been hard and even though I thought I had been, I was in no way ready for the arduous recovery I had to endure. The scars are huge too, with stitches running the whole length of my abdomen and the new boob being sewn on like a piece of patchwork quilt it was difficult to look at my body and remember what it had looked like pre cancer without all these garish scars. It was preferable to not having a breast, and my stomach looked flat, but I'm still undecided if the results outweigh the pain discomfort and scarring that it now has. It is amazing though to wake up and have a cleavage.

For anyone considering this surgery, I would urge you to visit your hospital where hopefully you can meet with ladies who have been through the operation and get to chat first hand about realistic expectations and what hopefully your end result may look like. My hospital in Devon holds a reconstruction evening for ladies twice a year. I found it to be invaluable. There is nothing like meeting someone and seeing the results in the flesh. No amount of internet searches will prepare you for that.

By all means join online discussion groups, Google photos; you can even see the operation on YouTube! There are ladies out there sharing their stories and showing their scars. This is so helpful and will help you to make up your mind. I would say the only question you really need to be asking yourself is: Do you have enough time to allow for recovery? Can you give yourself and can your family support you in a recovery that can last anywhere from four months to a year? If the answer is yes, then you can go for it! Prepare your home and family and get ready to be patient, as you will need to be very patient indeed.

Very slowly, my life started to return to normal. At twelve weeks I returned to swimming, managing only a few lengths the first time but building up slowly each time. I still had the abdominal pain and the swelling belly after I had done too much. It was difficult to gauge it just right. Some days I would be fine and others I would be in agony and not want to do a lot. I listened to my body and went with the flow. The following is a guide to what I was doing at each week and it gives you an idea what to expect. I also joined an online DIEP reconstruction closed group forum where I found all sorts of invaluable information and made a few new online friends.

Week 1: Hospital

Week 2: Home and bed rest. A trip to the toilet wore me out. I needed help dressing and washing. I still had three drains in, draining about 50-70 mm of fluid. The district nurse came in each day. I slept most of the time.

Week 3: I was able to wash and dress myself but still couldn't reach my toes or wash my own hair. Everything was getting slightly easier but I was still taking heavy pain relief and laxatives. I had all my drains removed, which made it much easier to sleep but I was still unable to do much without being worn out or in pain. Resting the majority of the time.

Week 4: I made it outside for a walk on the beach, but was still in bed most of the time. I was able to wash my own hair at last! I could wear my jeans again, but for only a few hours at a time. Abdomen still painful.

Week 5: I made it around the supermarket, still slow but getting better each day. I could make easy meals, lay the table and unload the dishwasher and was spending more time awake, only resting in the afternoon.

Week 6: I got out every day for a bit of fresh air, feeling good and resting when needed. Jeans were more comfortable and I was able to wear them all day. They actually helped to hold me together! All my scars were healing well with no open wounds. I managed to stay awake past nine o'clock at night, although I still liked to lie flat as it helped with the swelling at the end of the day.

Week 7: I was still sore and scared my stitches might split but I managed to be intimate. Wasn't very good as I was terrified my new boob would become detached or my stomach would burst open but it was a start - and you've got to start somewhere!

Week 8: I drove for the first time. I came to a roundabout and sneezed at the same time; boy was I glad I had waited until I healed!

Week 9: I went into town shopping on my own for the first time. Felt liberating!

Week 10: I caught the National Express to London to visit my son and daughter. We went to Harry Potter world and although I was tired I had a wonderful week going out every day.

Week 11: The previous week had worn me out so I spent most of it catching up with rest, early nights and healthy eating.

Week 12: I was back at Exeter hospital to schedule my next operation. Booked in for July 6th for a reduction to my good boob and uplift.

My surgeon had a good look at me and felt my scar tissue thoroughly, examining my new breast and my good one and declared that I was healing well.

'I still have the swelling on my abdomen,' I said, showing her my lump. However, after an ultrasound, it was decided that it was just swelling where the flap had been raised from and it was going to take a long time to heal. She asked me what was the worst thing about the op, and I had to think; already it seemed like a long time ago.

'It was the stooping over to walk, you bend over to ease the tummy pain but end up with back ache as you can't straighten up,' I said. 'It was like medieval torture and I had my moments when I had wondered what the hell I had put myself through.'

She wanted to know if it had been tougher than I expected.

'Definately!' I told her, 'I thought I had been prepared but I had no idea just how hard it would be.'

Finally, she asked what advice would I give to other patients contemplating the operation.

'To be as fit as you possibly can be, both physically and emotionally, and to have a good support structure behind you. This isn't something that you can do on your own,' I said, smiling at Terry and taking his hand, 'I couldn't have done this without him.'

Epilogue

* * *

I have just undergone my last surgery. Or I hope it will be my last one.

My good boob has been under the knife; it has been cut up, rearranged, and sewn back together. My nipple has been taken off, trimmed and sewn back into place too. The surgery was only a few hours long and before I knew it I was back on the ward. Almost two years to the day since I was first diagnosed I have had my good boob reduced and uplifted to match my new Barbie boob. I call it this, as at the moment it still doesn't have a nipple. I'm pleased with my DIEP results and glad I went through it as now with a bra or bikini on you can't tell it's not a real breast.

I bought the pyjamas - pink ones this time - and matching pink fluffy slippers with little pink bows on. I've sort of come to love the colour and embrace it. Well, you have to don't you? After all, isn't that what breast cancer is all about? I have my application form in front of me for next year's Race for Life. I am determined to be part of it and raise awareness and hopefully some money too for such a good cause.

Before I could put it all behind me I still had to have my follow-up check and so, a week after my operation, I was back at Exeter hospital having my dressings changed and to get the first peep at my new right boob. I'm so excited to see what it looks like and in my excitement completely forget that my breast tissue had been sent away for analysis. My histology has come back I'm told, and it seems my brush with breast cancer may not be over quite as soon as I'd hoped. The LCIS (Lobular Carcinoma in Situ) and calcifications that were spotted on my first mammogram have been found again on the tissue that they removed.

This time, however, the LCIS is what is called classic, and until it turns to pleomorphic I'm not in any trouble. This, I am told, could happen next year or in ten or twenty years' time. The most important bit is to keep going for my annual mammograms and if I find anything I am worried about I am to contact my breast care nurse immediately. I'm told that I can't rule out having to have another mastectomy - at some point.

The most important thing, my wonderful Reassuring Breast Care Nurse tells me, is to live life in the present. And that, my dear friends, is exactly what I am attempting to do. But, as anyone who has received the dreaded words, 'you have breast cancer' knows, this is easier said than done. The dread was here again, not holding me back, but not letting me move forward as fast as I was hoping to. The upcoming mammogram would be the new base line, I was told. It would show up (hopefully) what was going on and what treatment would be needed, either now or later. I was back to waiting, back to worrying, back to embracing my best friends: anxiety and fear.

I would be lying if I said I wasn't scared. This time I knew what might be ahead.

All I could think of was those appointments and tests. It had seemed never ending, sometimes the only things on our calendar were hospital appointments. Terry had been amazing, holding my hand every step of the way, but I could see the dread in his eyes and I couldn't bear to see him go through it all again with me. The doctors and nurses had been wonderful to me, but he had had little support. All my appointments were addressed to me and I knew he sometimes felt like a spare part when he was brushed aside or not talked to.

It had been hard for me, knowing the man I love was watching me go through an agony of treatments while he stood on the periphery. There isn't a lot of help for loved ones and as they end up becoming the main carer, I do feel it would help if they were made more part of the process, as without them then where would we be? Our beloved family and friends who accompany us to these rendezvous and keep us calm, the unsung heroes of our care and recovery should be so much more part of the whole package. I just desperately didn't want either of us to have to go through it all again, but mainly my anxiety was how Terry would cope.

I had stumbled through my original diagnosis in a baptism of fire, but this time I had insider knowledge of that road once trodden. This time I really did think, *This is it. My time's up.*

I cried out to Terry that my boobs would surely kill me, and for a few weeks felt like I was living with a ticking time bomb. I phoned my breast care nurse again – just in case they had got it wrong – just in case they had got mixed up.

I asked if I was right to be afraid, was I wrong to be worried sick? My Reassuring Breast Care Nurse explained all the findings again and, listening to her, I agreed with what had been said, but couldn't help adding, 'But we've been here before, remember?' It was like déjà vu. I couldn't shake off the thought that at last, I had the most beautiful breast but, like a naughty child at Christmas, I was in danger of having my new present taken away. I looked at my right boob constantly, felt it, and checked it for lumps or any other outward signs of disease. I got Terry to check it, as well as asking my mum, my daughter... I think if the postman had knocked on the door I would have asked him to have a feel too! Only a few weeks out of surgery, it was impossible to tell if there was anything wrong. The soft tissue had been mangled and stitched and so there would obviously be bruising and possible dried blood inside my breast, there was no way at this early stage that a breast exam could tell me anything, I had to sit patiently, recover and wait. I spoke to friends who were nurses and they told me I wasn't being silly and urged me to get my mammogram as soon as possible and demand to see my oncologist.

At six weeks my boob was healing well and I thought I could just about endure the pain of a mammogram. I phoned to see when my annual examination would be, as it was by now a few weeks overdue. Two weeks later and still no news, despite being told an appointment would be sent out in the post to me, so I phoned yet again. This time there were no records of me needing a mammogram. It turned out that as I had been working away in Lincoln last year, and had had my first annual mammogram at Lincoln County Hospital, I wasn't on the register at Exeter anymore! Eventually, I was told a request would be put in and, hopefully, I would receive my appointment in the next couple of weeks. My surgeon was the one person who could authorize my mammogram and the card requesting this was sitting in her in tray. Unfortunately for me she was sitting on a beach somewhere in the Mediterranean and had no idea of my dilemma. There was only one thing for it: I had to wait. Until my surgeon returned from her holiday in two weeks' time there was nothing anyone could do. I could hardly contain my annoyance. Despite trying, I was finding it hard living in the present.

Eventually after countless sleepless nights, rolling around with hot sweats and insomnia, I phoned my doctor to see if she could help. I had a feeling the anxiety of the upcoming mammogram was to blame and until I had that under my belt I knew I would be thinking the worst. I was finding it hard to shake off this black cloud that was hanging over my head. I knew I should be looking on the bright side, but somehow I just couldn't find my positive pants. Agreeing with me, she was happy to help; she prescribed me sleeping tablets. Knowing what I might be facing again, she understood my fear. Sympathetic and supportive, my wonderful doctor asked if she could do anything else for me so I told her about my discomfort down below.

'That will be the Tamoxifen,' she replied.

The hormone repellent tablet that I would be on for five to ten years was causing my oestrogen levels to plummet and along with it my sex drive.

'I can prescribe a few things,' she said, 'I'll make you a goody bag up of lubricants and creams, there is a very good one called 'Yes! Yes! Yes!' you might like.'

Thanking her I said, 'I think Terry might like the sound of that, as it's been a bit, 'no, no, no' lately.'

'Well, let's face it Karen, she told me, 'you've got enough on your plate; there's no need to have a lousy love life too.' I thought she made a good point.

The following day when I went to collect my goody bag, one of the items was missing. The pharmacist exclaimed that it needed to be ordered in especially for me.
As I entered The Chemist Shop the following day, the receptionist exclaimed.

'Ah, Karen Bates, your prescription is here.'

I asked, 'How do you know my name?' to which she replied that some people have familiar faces. I arrived home and put my package on the table, opening up the paper bag, I said to Terry, 'I think someone has been having a laugh at my expense,' as I put the tube of 'Yes! Yes! Yes!' in his hand.

*

And so, as I sit here finishing off this book, waiting on yet more tests, I'm reminded that although the pink ladies club is not a club anyone wants to join, you can be assured that there are hundreds if not thousands of women out there who have got your back.

If it turns out that I am going to need further treatment, then I can be sure that one of my online friends will have done it before me and with her knowledge and guidance I will be able to relax a little knowing I will get to the other side just as she has done.

As I turn to my online buddies for reassurance and hope that my journey isn't starting all over again. I'm reminded that they are there for me, as we all support each other and everyone else supports us; I'm reminded of the sisterhood of care I am so very much a part of. We need each other, whether we have been diagnosed today, or twenty years ago. Yes, it's with us forever, we will always be members of the pink ladies club, but hopefully for most of us it will become a smaller aspect of our lives and as we go on to grow old we can be there for anyone starting down this path, with wise words and wisdom and a gentle knowledge that we have trodden those steps that you have suddenly found yourself travelling on.

There is help, and there is always, always, hope.

Resources

Macmillan Cancer Support
www.macmillan.org.uk
Fantastic for all sorts of information and they have a free phone number to call if you or a loved one needs to talk. Monday to Friday, 9am – 8pm, **0808 808 00 00**

Breast cancer now
www.breastcancernow.org
The UK's leading breast cancer research charity

Chemo Hero
Registered charity based in North Devon
Providing kindness in a box to patients receiving chemotherapy in North Devon.
Founded by Lisa Wallis.
www.chemohero.com

FORCE Cancer Charity Royal Devon and Exeter Hospital
Support and information centre for anyone facing cancer

Over and Above Charity
Overandabove.org.uk
Raising funds to build a purpose build cancer centre for North Devon

Knitted Knockers UK

A registered charity providing prosthesis to mastectomy patients.
You can find them online or via Facebook to request your knitted or aqua knocker.

Drain Dollies

These are bags to hold your drains in, they're canvas and hide the drain and its contents and also make it less likely to forget you have one in and pull it – you only do that once!
Again, you can find these on an Internet search. I was lucky and my hospital provided them for me. You can find them on Facebook.

Mastectomy Cushions

Jens friends' mastectomy pillows are perfect. The pillows are used after mastectomy / any breast surgery to help support and protect the sensitive chest area. They help by fitting under the arm when doing everyday tasks such as sitting, sleeping, watching TV and when in the car. You can find them on Facebook.

UK Breast Cancer support group for sufferers and survivors is a closed Facebook group for   anyone facing breast cancer.

You need never be alone.

Acknowledgments:

* * *

Thank you to all, friends, family, healthcare professionals and fellow pink ladies.
Your love, kindness and support has been very gratefully received.
A massive hug goes out to each and everyone of you.

I would like to give a particular mention to my husband Terry, my children; Sarah and Ashley and my Mum and Dad. I don't know how I would have gotten through this without you all.

With special thanks to the following for being there for me, with messages, texts, cards, presents, advice and constant support:
Elaine Morris,
Juliet Doyle,
Heather Myatt,
Claire Walker,
Stella Brown.

A big thank you also to Sarah Dawes, for editing and whipping the pink ladies club into shape.
Dawn Peters, my reassuring breast care nurse.
Laura Hanson, my chemo nurse and friend.
Sheena McBryde of Lincoln Permanent makeup, for giving me back my eyebrows, paid for with a smile.
Lisa Wallis for her kindness. A true chemo hero!

And everyone else who took the time to like my posts on Facebook, sent me encouraging messages and didn't get fed up with me going on about breast cancer.

You are all in my heart forever.

About the author

$$* * *$$

Karen Bates is an author who credits her writing to a hobby, which 'got out of hand.'

She lives in Devon with her husband Terry where they enjoy kayaking, learning to Salsa and watching Star Trek.

You can follow Karen and find out more about her and her writing on Facebook: /karen.bates.7393 and twitter: @KarenBates64 where she would love to hear from you.

Printed in Great Britain
by Amazon